LIKE FATHER, LIKE SON

Ernest Manning and Preston Manning

140201

Lloyd Mackey

ECW PRESS

CANADIAN CATALOGUING IN PUBLICATION DATA

Mackey, Lloyd
Like father, like son: Ernest Manning and Preston Manning

ISBN 1-55022-299-6

1. Manning, Ernest C., 1908–1996. 2. Manning, Preston, 1942–   .
3. Christianity and politics. 4. Prime Ministers – Alberta –
Biography. 5. Politicians – Canada – Biography.   I. Title

FC601.AIM32 1997   971.06′092′2   C96-932470-7
F1034.3.A2M32 1997

Design and imaging by ECW Type & Art, Oakville, Ontario.
Printed by Imprimerie Gagné, Louiseville, Quebec.

Distributed in Canada by General Distribution Services,
30 Lesmill Road, Don Mills, Ontario M3B 2T6.

Distributed in the United States by General Distribution Services,
85 River Rock Drive, Suite 202, Buffalo, New York 14207.

Published by ECW PRESS,
2120 Queen Street East, Suite 200,
Toronto, Ontario M4E 1E2.

http://www.ecw.ca/press

To Phyllis Mackey
and the late Stephen Mackey,
my parents,
who created the environment,
half a century ago,
that eventually led to the
writing of this book.

Table of Contents

List of Illustrations

Acknowledgements

I would like to acknowledge the following for their help in making this book possible.

- The University of Alberta Archives and the Alberta Provincial Museum and Archives, both in Edmonton. The U of A Archives is the repository of the tapes and transcripts of oral interviews conducted in the early 1980s by Lydia Semotuk. In some cases, because the quotations used were transcribed verbatim from the tapes, I have edited them for written clarity. I have tried, as much as possible, to keep the meaning of those quotations true to the original transcripts. The Provincial Museum and Archives is the repository of the Premier's Papers; the collection contains a large number of letters from both the Aberhart and Manning eras, as well as many relevant newspaper and magazine clippings.
- Ernest Manning and Preston and Sandra Manning for the time they spent with me, at various intervals, in both formal interviews and informal conversations. Preston and Sandra have been most helpful in the fact-checking process, as well as in making available the photos included in the book.
- Jean Marie Cleminger and Ian Todd from Preston Manning's staff in Ottawa, who have helped to fill in many of the knowledge gaps and to facilitate contacts with Preston.
- Jack David and Dallas Harrison, my editors at ECW Press, who have helped me to turn this stream-of-consciousness document into reader-friendly narrative. Dallas's familiarity with the prairie religious and political scene added to the technical

side of the editorial process, as a check on my own insights.

- Roy Bell and Howard Bentall, two distinguished retired Baptist ministers who spent part of their tenure in Alberta and saw both the faith and the political backdrops of the book's subjects from an arm's-length perspective.
- John Barr, Don Braid, Murray Dobbin, Alvin Finkel, Tom Flanagan, and Sidney Sharpe, who have all written extensively about either Ernest or Preston Manning. Dobbin and Finkel, particularly, have written from viewpoints quite opposite to those held by the Mannings. The leftward lean of their writings served to hold me in check, so that my rather sympathetic approach could be kept in balance.
- My wife, Edna, whose abilities as an administrator and whose care for me have made it possible for me to take the time needed to write this book.

Unless otherwise noted, all photos are courtesy of Preston and Ernest Manning.

Introduction

ERNEST MANNING ascended to both the premiership of Alberta and the radio pulpit of Canada's national *Back to the Bible Hour* in 1943, at the age of thirty-four. It had been just a year since his wife, Muriel, had given birth to Preston, the second of their two sons.

Over the mountains and across Georgia Strait, in Victoria, a boy of three was completely unaware of those seemingly far-off events. Within a decade, though, I was to undergo my political coming of age.

My father was a firefighter and my mother was a homemaker. I had a brother a tad younger than Preston Manning and a sister who was born in 1949. Our parents were devout members of Oaklands Gospel Hall, part of a loosely knit group of churches collectively nicknamed the Christian Brethren or Plymouth Brethren. Faith, not politics, was their main agenda.

Around 1951, having been given the family five-tube table radio after my parents splurged on a new Chisholm radio-phonograph, I began listening on Sunday afternoons to some of the radio preachers whose names were sometimes mentioned in church. Most of them, like Billy Graham, Charles E. Fuller, Walter Maier, and Myron F. Boyd, were American. But one afternoon I discovered that there was a Canadian in the crowd — no less than the premier of Alberta.

13

Coincidentally, the political party led by that premier, Social Credit, was emerging as a force to be reckoned with in British Columbia. Not a few of my parents' friends believed that *Back to the Bible Hour* was a significant factor in the spread of Social Credit over the mountains, even though Premier Manning stuck pretty much to the Bible and refrained from direct political references during his radio sermons.

In 1951, now approaching my teens, I persuaded my parents to take the family vacation in Seattle and Vancouver. Billy Graham was to preach in the Seattle High School Memorial Stadium. In Vancouver, Premier Manning (as he was reverentially referred to in our home) had a radio rally scheduled in a hockey rink called The Forum. I wanted to hear my radio heroes in person.

A few months later, having been taught tithing — giving ten percent of my earnings to God — I sent $1.23 from my *Victoria Times* paper-route earnings to the premier. A kindly letter arrived in our home just days later, thanking me for the money and quoting from Ecclesiastes 11.1, which reads: "Cast your bread upon the waters, and it will return to you after many days."

The years passed, and I grew to young manhood, attending Bible college, serving short pastoral internships, and shifting into journalism. In 1979, I was assigned by *Decision*, the magazine published by Billy Graham, to interview the premier, who was now a senator. I reminded Senator Manning of his reference to "bread upon the waters." His reply, with a mischievous look in an otherwise grave, dignified, and slightly wrinkled face, was "Well, perhaps the bread is returning to you today." *Decision* ran the story as a preface to a Billy Graham crusade in Edmonton, for which the former premier served as honorary chairman. After one of the Graham meetings, the senator introduced me to his elder son, Preston.

As the years passed, Preston and Sandra kept in touch with me and my wife, Edna. In 1986, during a lunch meeting, Preston pulled some papers out of his briefcase and showed them to me. The papers described plans for a new political party, called Reform. Three years later, I began a two-year contract stint as editor of the party's newspaper, the *Reformer*.

Ernest Manning once told me that, when he was too old and weak to do anything else, he would write his memoirs. When he died on 19 February 1996, he left a fine set of premier's papers at the Alberta provincial archives. And he had been extensively taped in the early 1980s by Lydia Semotuk, then a University of Alberta student. But he never wrote those memoirs.

My own faith and political pilgrimage have permitted me to observe the Mannings in an unusual manner. I have been able to trace the points where faith and politics converge and to compare and contrast father and son, utilizing the faith-politics matrix to explore the complexities of their relationship and their influence on each other. Ernest Manning never served in opposition; Preston Manning, to this point, has not sat in government. Those facts represent one of the striking contrasts between the two.

I trust that this exploration of the Mannings will help Canadians to understand the many ways in which faith and political experience interplay. Some readers will enjoy the political aspects of the Manning story but find the religious parts to be something they would sooner ignore. I invite such readers to accompany me through the parts of the book that portray the evangelical Christian subculture. It is a significant part of what Canada is about, and is often trivialized in mainstream Canadian journalism. There is a sense of community in Canadian evangelicalism that runs deep and warm. Furthermore, the politics of evangelicalism are both complex and essential in the informal effectiveness of its community.

Some pundits interpret the Manning story as a case of church interfering in the affairs of state. In so doing, they misunderstand the impact of one's belief system on life and in the case of a politician — politics. In researching the Manning story, I was intrigued to discover some parallels between faith and politics on the political left, as well as in the political "establishment" in central and eastern Canada. Please watch for those side trips. I hope they will help to place the Mannings in context.

Like Father, Like Son should not be seen as a comprehensive history of either Reform or Social Credit. It is meant to highlight the events that relate most directly to Ernest and Preston Manning, the father and the son.

CHAPTER I

Apprenticing with "Bible Bill"

THE STORY of Ernest and Preston Manning requires the backdrop created by another relationship — that involving Ernest Manning and William "Bible Bill" Aberhart. And not completely unrelated was the rise, in one province to the east, of a Baptist minister named Tommy Douglas.

Several biographers have referred to the Manning-Aberhart student-mentor rapport as being just one step short of a father-son association. And it began with a desire by a teenage Manning to plug in to the new age of radio. In 1925, living with his parents on their homestead near the tiny community of Rosetown, Saskatchewan, 150 kilometres southwest of Saskatoon, he spent his savings on an Emerson radio that showed promise of picking up the weakest signals from the ionosphere. One Sunday afternoon, he discovered *Back to the Bible Hour* and the passionate fundamentalist preaching of William Aberhart.

Ernest Manning's parents, good United Church folk, were not particularly pious. Aberhart's intense and serious exposition of the Bible was a stark contrast to his family's more "take it as it comes" approach to faith. Particularly intriguing to the young Ernest was the preacher's way of relating ancient biblical texts to current events.

Aberhart was not a clergyman by profession but a public school principal. He was known to be a fine teacher and a diligent administrator, but his passion for the Bible — particularly its prophetic passages — was legendary. In whatever church he attended, he was active. Indeed, his leadership was domineering in style, often causing friction between him and the minister, or the congregation, or both.

By the time Manning heard him on the radio, Aberhart was laying plans for the fulfilment of a dream. He wanted to start a Bible school in which an emphasis on the prophetic approach could be freely developed. That dream came to fruition in 1927, when the Calgary Prophetic Bible Institute, which had been run as an evening school since 1918, began day classes. And Ernest Manning was one of the first full-time students. The radio preacher's passion had reached deep into the heart of the teenager, causing him to commit his life to Christ.

That commitment was a quiet enough act. There was no rolling on the floor or shouting with ecstasy — acts often inaccurately attributed to an evangelical style of conversion. Manning was always a very orderly person, and such behaviour would have been out of character. And it was not Aberhart's emphasis on biblical prophecy that reached Manning but his declaration that God loved people so much that, in the person of his son, Jesus, he had come to earth to live and ultimately to die. And that death was to effect the redemption of people who had sinned, lost their way, and wandered from God. Even before heading to Calgary in 1927, Ernest Manning nurtured his new faith with regular study of the Bible.

William Aberhart, an Ontario transplant, moved to Alberta in 1911. His move was motivated by a desire to go west and try his hand at a new life. Ontario was not seen as the land of golden opportunity at the time, while western Canada had been opening up for forty years since Confederation. Indeed, Alberta had only moved from territorial status to provincehood six years before the rotund young schoolteacher, his fun-loving wife, Jessie, and their two daughters, Khona and Ola, arrived in Calgary.

Aberhart's early religious life was Presbyterian. From his earliest years, he was a student of scripture. While preparing at the University of Toronto for his teaching career, he taught a Bible class. It was there that his dramatic style of delivery was honed. That style enabled him to excel in the public school classroom, in church pulpits, and later in the political arena. He would begin speaking quietly enough, but his voice would rise to a crescendo. His jowls would shake, and his eyes would enflame as he punctuated his speech with finger-pointing and podium-slamming. He was, in short, a spellbinder.

His workaholism threatened to engulf him at times, especially during the 1920s, when he was simultaneously principal of Crescent Heights High School, leading elder at Westbourne Baptist Church, principal of the Calgary Prophetic Bible Institute, and speaker on what later became known as *Canada's National Bible Hour*. Indeed, the Calgary school board occasionally tried to rein Aberhart in, suggesting that teaching the school curriculum by day and the Bible by night was bound to wear him out — not to mention placing him in a potentially severe conflict of interest. But no one was ever successful at gathering enough evidence that his Bible and church activities adversely impacted on his "main job."

In those early days, Aberhart invariably ended his radio programs with a compelling invitation to his listeners to consider the claims of Christ, to accept him as saviour and own him as Lord of their lives. Ernest Manning accepted that invitation, and it changed the course of his life. He began studying the Bible and, in fact, could not get enough of it. Years later, he was fond of recalling that plowing the fields on his father's farm worked well for his scripture study. The furrows were long, and he could get a fair amount of memory work done before having to turn the tractor around.

When the autumn of 1927 arrived, Manning was in Calgary, ready to continue his Bible education at Calgary Prophetic. At that time, one would have been hard put to get into a deep conversation with the young student about politics. He was being steeped in esoteric biblical subjects such as Old Testament survey, homiletics, hermeneutics, and systematic theology.

By contrast, when his son Preston sought higher education twenty-five years later, he took three years of physics at the University of Alberta before switching to economics. He never had any formal theological education.

But for the senior Manning, the studies represented only one facet of the learning curve on which he found himself. Aberhart saw in the young man a person who could greatly assist him. Aberhart became Manning's mentor, and Manning, in turn, emerged as Aberhart's trusted assistant. For several months, Manning even lived in the Aberhart home. At Calgary Prophetic, the work included running the office, preparing schedules, and generally handling the minutiae that Aberhart had no time to deal with. After completing the course of studies, Manning's work grew into a full-time job.

Manning developed another reason to keep closely connected with the school and Aberhart's radio program. That reason was Muriel Preston, the pianist. The two became good friends, and the course of romance grew into love. It was not until after Manning was in politics, however, that the pair married. Premier Aberhart, having assumed the surrogate parental role for both sides in the new partnership, "gave away" the bride.

Manning was a serious student of the Aberhart style, as well as a loyal aide and a prodigious worker. However, he was developing his own style — an approach to politics, relationships, and problem-solving that would come into its own once he became Alberta's premier.

Manning and Aberhart met just before the Depression and the prairie drought of the late 1920s and early 1930s hit. That combination of economic and natural disasters caused the two to ponder the potential impact of some of the biblical prophecies to which they were committed. In particular, they wondered whether biblical doctrine could provide solutions to the problems of poverty, misery, and hunger.

Around the same time, a young man named Tommy Douglas was preparing to become a Baptist minister. On completion of his studies, he became the pastor of a church in Weyburn, Saskatchewan. Like Manning, he had committed his life to Christ as a teenager. And, as a young minister, he also wondered how the Christian gospel could address the very real struggles that prairie people were facing as a result of the Depression and drought. Undoubtedly, the schools that Manning and Douglas respectively attended shaped the ways in which each would relate faith and politics in later years.

Calgary Prophetic was a fundamentalist school that, in some ways, was a reaction to the social gospel and "modernism" that were sweeping Protestant denominations in the 1910s and 1920s. It was one of many Bible schools and institutes scattered across the prairies. They took what was described by theologians as a "high view" of scripture, believing it to be the only and complete written word of God. And they were sceptical of pastors and teachers who tried to turn the Bible into a tool to address social issues. They saw the social gospel as a capitulation by Christians to the inroads of socialism.

For his part, Douglas took his ministerial training at Brandon College, a school operated by the Baptist Union of Western Canada. It tended toward the social gospel approach. Indeed, at the time that churches and denominations were splitting over the fundamentalist-modernist argument, Brandon and the Baptist Union sided — albeit with some reservations — with the modernist side. Baptist Union ministerial candidates were being taught to see the Christian gospel as a gadfly to the established order. This view provided a chance to correct poverty or address some other social issues.

Bible Bill, by David R. Elliott and Iris Miller, documents Aberhart's involvement in the fundamentalism-modernism controversy that wracked North American Protestantism. In short, the issue was the modernist contention that the Bible is something less than the inerrant word of God that the fundamentalists maintained it was.

Some of Aberhart's prophetic preaching, in fact, hinted at the eschatological basis for his views. He interpreted the seven churches featured in Revelation to be the various Canadian denominations — such as Baptist, Presbyterian, United, Anglican, Lutheran, and Roman Catholic. His favourite was the church at Ephesus — the Baptists, he believed — followed closely by the church at Smyrna, the Presbyterians. And he was very concerned about the 1925 formation of the United Church, which took in a portion of the Presbyterian denomination. The most "apostate" church in Revelation was Sardis, which he identified as the United group.

The Baptists' involvement in the fundamentalist-modernist controversy had an impact on the pathway Aberhart took. Although in a church that, at the time, was affiliated with the Baptist Union of Western Canada, he declared that the group's Brandon College was on the modernist side. During some of his early Alberta years he was at Calgary's prestigious Grace Presbyterian Church. Later, he affiliated himself with Westbourne Baptist Church, an offshoot of Grace's eminent rival, First Baptist. And Westbourne, in due course and under his influence, separated itself from the Baptist Union — obviously ready to stand for a fundamentalist approach to the Christian faith.

As Aberhart pondered all these issues, he was introduced to the theories of Major C.H. Douglas. A British teacher, Douglas was advocating Social Credit as the answer to Depression-spawned economic woes. In brief, Douglas taught that the banking system was corrupt and that governments needed to develop radical monetary reforms that would, in effect, bypass the banks. Governments would issue "social credit" instead of currency, in exchange for certain human endeavours. Such a system, he suggested, would enable nations to pull themselves out of economic depressions.

Aberhart studied these theories carefully and began weaving them into his *Bible Hour* radio programs and his Calgary Prophetic lectures. Indeed, he became adept at mixing biblical interpretation with political, economic, and social theory at every possible opportunity. And the Social Credit theory was a winner in terms of its public appeal. With the network established through the radio program, he began developing Social Credit study groups, and they flourished throughout the province. The interest in Social Credit exploded. At the same time, a vacuum of trust among voters had developed over allegations of an illicit sexual liaison made against the United Farmers' premier, J.R. Brownlee.

Aberhart, often accompanied by Manning, would accept speaking engagements, in small Alberta towns, triggered by the Social Credit content in his radio sermons. Manning

6

omit in this ring

Mr. Manning's first lecture on Social Credit.

Strathcona
~~Edmonton~~ East Con'sty Meeting. King Edward Park Community Hall.

The basic things with which we are concerned –

1 Production
2 Distribution
3 Consumption.

Four Essential Factors:

1 Raw Materials (in Alberta we have a tremendous variety – our standard of
            living is limited only by the maximum amount of raw
                                            Materials)
2 Skill and Initiative
3 Physical facilities
4 Money (the financial system)

Categories of capital necessary to the economy of the nation.

1. Industrial Capital: Necessary to provide plants and equipment for proces-
            sing of raw material. Mostly private and corporation
            investment. It is good for individuals to have a
            stake in the means of production.

2. Operating capital: Maintenance, wages, salaries etc. Mostly bank loans.

3. Social Capital: Necessary to provide hospitals, schools, public and
            municipal buildings. Should come from Bank of
            Canada at very low interest rate.

4. Capital for Social Services:
            O.A.Pensions, other penstions, hospital and medical
            Services, welfare services – Now provided by taxation –
            formerly by individual, family or local community.

Consumer Purchasing Power. Wages, salaries, pensions etc. Should equal the
            total prices of-
All Products of Industry: Purchasing power is seldom as high as total prices
            (except in war-time when we sometimes have more
            (money than goods – hence inflation.) Additional
            (credit should make up this difference.)

Good Economy-   is when consumer purchasing power equals the total
            value of all products of nation.(goods & services)

Vicious Circle   No purchasing power – cause of depression.
            Too much money, too few goods – cause of inflation.

Price Levels   We are now in an abnormally high price level. Not as
            good as low price level because it adversely affects
            fixed incomes.

Social Credit   If purchasing power is not equal to prices it is the
            duty of the government to expand purchasing power.
            Redundant credit must be withdrawn to balance. Purchas-
            ing power should never be enlarged beyond the total
            value of goods. Consumer dividend is the direct method
            of putting more money into circulation.

1. Notes prepared for Ernest Manning's first
lecture on Social Credit, before the 1935 election
that brought the party to power in Alberta.

later recalled that some of those "town meetings" were held in outdoor locales that would accommodate the largest possible crowds. In towns of two hundred, for example, audiences of two thousand — pouring in from the surrounding rural areas — would plant themselves on piles of lumber in building supply yards.

When the results of the 22 August 1935 election came in, Social Credit was in power. But Aberhart himself had not been a candidate and did not take a seat in the legislature until after a by-election in Okotoks/High River. Manning was appointed provincial secretary — Aberhart having developed a healthy respect for the young man's loyalty and attention to detail. It was a post that would serve Manning well in preparing him to assume the premiership eight years later.

The first Social Credit term was marked by a number of daring legislative initiatives. Some of the most controversial related to attempts to rein in the "fifty big shots" from central Canada. Prairie populism always involved a sense of grievance toward the power brokers of central Canada. The banks were targets — and, indeed, the whole Social Credit ideology was based on developing a homegrown autonomous financial system.

Aberhart wanted to rein in the press as well, and some of his legislation in that respect was probably what gave him a reputation, in his later years, of moving distinctly leftward. His moves on the press came in two forms: a bill of censorship and, later, an attempt to have the Social Credit Party buy the *Albertan*, Calgary's second paper. The legislation was one of several ruled to be ultra vires during his tenure; the paper-buying attempt just wouldn't fly. Manning recalled in later years that Aberhart was so frustrated with the opposition he experienced from the major papers that he believed it hampered the ability of government to get the strong and radical legislation that was needed.

Manning tended to distance himself from the Aberhart hyperbole, all the while indicating that he understood. For his own part, some of his strongest language in the archival interviews was saved for what he described as so-called investigative reporting. While he had no problem with reporters digging for the facts, he thought that some used the mask of "investigative journalism" to carry out agendas of character assassination.

Interestingly, one group that seemed to warm to Aberhart toward the end of his time was organized labour — possibly because labour leaders saw him as being capable of struggling alongside them, against the same establishment and corporate giants.

Two letters written shortly before Aberhart's death and now contained in the premier's archives give some clue to the state of his relationships at the time. One, from Carl E. Berg, secretary of the Alberta Federation of Labour, and dated 22 May 1943, expressed regret at Aberhart's illness, noting:

> As you know, I was opposed to him in the beginning, but I have learned to love and respect him, as in all his dealings, he has been more than fair to me and the people I represent. And I have, for a long time, contended that he is the best premier in Canada.

And, on 14 April of the same year, Aberhart wrote to a critic — one claiming to be a fellow Christian who had converted to Christ in 1936. He noted: "In my opinion, no sincere man could ever write a letter such as you have written unless someone had upset him or he was distressed by an evil spirit in some way." Apparently, the writer, Vernon Barber of Calgary, had levelled some financially based accusations at Aberhart. His response:

2. Cartoonists enjoyed poking fun at the relationship between William Aberhart and his "apprentice," Ernest Manning. This Stewart Cameron cartoon in the 5 August 1939 *Calgary Herald* depicted their efforts to publish a book on Social Credit achievements entitled *The Record Tells the Story.*

You say I have defrauded the people by taking their money under false pretences. I have never received money from the people for preaching the Gospel and so how could you make that charge? Any preaching I do is done gratis and how do you make out that I have sold my birthright for a mess of pottage?

(The "mess of pottage" reference is drawn from the biblical story of Esau, Isaac's older son, who, in great hunger, sold his birthright to Isaac's younger brother, Jacob, in exchange for a mess of pottage. More current Bible translations use the term "bowl of lentils.")

That letter, intriguingly, was written two days after a note to Cyril Hutchinson, one of Aberhart's church colleagues, saying that Aberhart was so weak that he could not be at church that Sunday. There is a hint of some possible controversy shaping up, because he says: "I thought I would let you know early so that you could prepare yourself for the ordeal."

In the early months of 1943, William Aberhart grew progressively weaker. He and his family headed for Vancouver so that he could recuperate, but he never returned to Calgary. He died on 23 May of cirrhosis of the liver.

Ernest Manning had watched, from close range, a take-over bid by people in the Social Credit Party — known as the "insurgents" — who felt that Aberhart was departing from Major Douglas's economic teachings. Now Manning was poised to take over the premiership of Alberta.

CHAPTER 2

Out on His Own

IN PREPARING TO WRITE about Ernest Manning's premiership, I read substantially from material about that period. Two strong and relevant works were *The Social Credit Phenomenon in Alberta* by Alvin Finkel, a labour specialist from Athabaska University, and *The Dynasty: The Rise and Fall of Social Credit in Alberta*, by John J. Barr. Finkel's work is a detailed account that tackles Manning's political career and administration from a left-leaning — some might suggest a Marxist — perspective. His analysis leaves the clear impression that Manning did not engage enough in interventionist politics. On the other hand, Barr, who was an administrative assistant to a Manning education minister, Robert Clark, has written a sympathetic account.

In tackling the tenure of Manning in the context of his relationship with his son, however, my account attempts to tie in, more closely than others have done, the relationship between religious faith and politics. The thesis on which my approach is predicated is that evangelicalism in Alberta was and is a moderate movement — conservative leaning and cautious, not hard right and radical. Furthermore, I contend that moderation permeated Ernest Manning's Social Credit Party and, later, Preston Manning's Reform Party, taking them toward the centre of the political spectrum. Thus, I relate the story in such a way as to move the reader back and forth between the religious and the political aspects of the Manning saga, all the while comparing and contrasting the ideas, styles, and experiences of the father and the son.

The apprenticeship of Ernest Manning having ended with the death of his mentor, William Aberhart, the "son" that Aberhart had never had was now ready to take over where his "father" had left off. There was just a little competition for the job, from cabinet colleague Solon Low, a Mormon. Low later went on to the national leadership of Social Credit, where he was succeeded ultimately by the evangelical Robert Thompson.

I mention the religious connections here to reinforce the fact that, in Social Credit, the religious beliefs of the key players were quite different from those that prevailed elsewhere. It would have been unthinkable, at the time, for Mormons or evangelical Christians to rise to the top of the political heap in other parts of Canada. Baptists, Plymouth Brethren, and Jehovah's Witnesses were being jailed in Maurice Duplessis's militantly Catholic Quebec. In Atlantic Canada, Ontario, and British Columbia, mainstream Protestants stood the best chance of election. And in British Columbia, the union movement was a strong "religious substitute" that kept the socialists close to the corridors of power.

During the war years, pacifist Mennonites were persecuted by "the English" who often believed that Mennonite farmers were benefiting from the fact that non-Mennonite farm youth were away fighting for their country. But in Alberta, those otherwise relegated by the establishment to religious oddballery were in the ascendancy. And under Manning, they would get the chance to prove that they could make the best parts of their faith contribute to good government.

Manning was loath to criticize his mentor. He acknowledged the debt he owed to Aberhart for bringing him along in the worlds of faith and politics. Manning believed in and practised loyalty, and that practice compelled him to be at Aberhart's beck and call. He was often called on to pinch-hit for the premier at a speaking engagement. As provincial secretary, he was expected to keep a close eye on both the movement of legislation through the house and the execution of cabinet orders-in-council. But there is a sense, from reading Manning's archival interviews and correspondence from his office, that the day he took over the premier's office he saw it as his duty to bring order out of chaos. (Preston Manning believes that, if Aberhart had lived, Social Credit in Alberta would have died.)

Aberhart was combative; Manning went out of his way to avoid arguments — but he was no patsy. Columnist Allan Fotheringham, interviewed on the CBC's *Pamela Wallin Live* on the day of Manning's funeral, said that people knew someone was in charge when Manning was premier. That is all the more remarkable when one considers that, at thirty-four, he was the youngest ever in Canada's history to assume a premiership. (When Preston was thirty-four, he was still virtually unknown to the public.)

Manning needed to grab the reins quickly in 1943. He did so with a no-nonsense approach, but he was also a listener and a problem-solver rather than an arguer. He trusted and affirmed people. By doing so, he won their loyalty to the cause of good government.

At the beginning of its tenure, Social Credit was on the fringes of the political process. There was a sense of mutual contempt between Aberhart's administration and the power brokers in central Canada. Indeed, Aberhart knew how to exploit that contempt to the voters' delight.

But Manning carefully built a base of rational decision-making that rendered Aberhart's combative style redundant. In the process, he muted many of the "screwballs" whom Aberhart had legitimized by arguing with them. By muting them, however, he really made them more useful. By listening to them and commending them for their willingness to express their views, he communicated that he was interested in where they were coming from. But he also let it be known that, in a democracy, one needed to listen to a wide range of people — not just those who believed they had a message from God.

When Manning called his first election for 8 August 1944, his party had thirty-five seats in the legislature. The 1940 election had been raucous. Aberhart had gone into power in 1935 with fifty-six out of sixty-three seats. Some of the legislation of the first term had been declared ultra vires by the courts. His attempt to restrict press freedom had won him some media enemies. So there had been much to fight over, and it had left Social Credit somewhat depleted.

But the 1944 election did not have Aberhart to kick around any more, so to speak. In his archival interviews, Manning notes:

> I am sure there were some [of Aberhart's critics] who had a few twinges that the viciousness of their attacks on him had contributed to his early death. . . . Now he was gone. This change gave an opportunity for any who had any doubts as to whether all of this had been quite fair and appropriate to change without losing face. I came along as a young person, a new face, a new government, and a new start.

Reiterating his great admiration for Aberhart's abilities and objectives, he recalls, however, that for Aberhart "there were no grey areas — it was black or white, you are for me or against me." For Manning, it was different:

32

My approach was not that way. I think I could be just as adamant in standing for what I felt was right and necessary, but I never got any satisfaction of making somebody mad if you could gain your end by more congenial means.

I have always thought there was a great deal of truth in the old philosophy that says the greatest victory you could have over any enemy is to make him your friend.

So cooperation, rather than antagonism, became the order of the day.

Business had been antagonistic to the Aberhart Socreds, largely because of his attacks on the banks. But Manning says business also knew that his party was in favour of free enterprise, so that community's antagonism lessened as the 1944 vote approached.

But another factor came into the equation. Manning successfully — and sincerely — communicated the idea that he was not "dying to be premier — and not married to the job." He was comfortable in office, but he was not compulsively beholden to it. In retrospect, he says, that turned out to be pretty good politics: "It is hard to throw someone out if he says 'I don't care if you throw me out or not, but as long as I am here I will do what I think is best for the province and country.' "

His rather casual desire to remain premier was no ruse. Many Albertans were aware that his first call had been to the Christian ministry. The route into politics had been a diversion. But Manning always held the view that both God and the people had some say in how long he would be premier — and he was not about to argue with either.

His son looks at things the same way. Will he ever be prime minister or the real leader of the opposition? Preston Manning, in political scientist and former Reform policy director Tom Flanagan's view, is not proactive enough in

33

pressing for a strongly ideological right-wing policy. In *Waiting for the Wave* Flanagan insists that must be done in order to provide a real niche for the party on the federal scene. But Preston is surprisingly laid-back on the question. Yes, he would like to be prime minister, but if the people — and God — do not want that, then there is not much he can do about it. And he will live with whatever happens.

There is a further point to ponder in Preston's approach. He often states that a true reconciler, in the Christian context, must be prepared for sacrifice for the sake of conflict resolution. For example, one senses that, if the greater cause of social conservatism requires a political coalescing of a new sort in the future, perhaps, as the reconciler, he will need to let someone else be prime minister.

But that does not stop him from cracking the whip occasionally on matters that might keep Reform from power. He did that in the spring of 1996, when he suspended two of his MPs from caucus for allegedly homophobic comments. At its assembly in Vancouver a few weeks later, he insisted that, if the Reform Party really wanted power, some of its members needed to shed seemingly bigoted attitudes. The point is that, for many of these questions, Preston Manning handles them much as his father would have forty years before. He believes in turning enemies into friends.

Social Credit's reputation for anti-Semitism was also an issue that Ernest Manning tackled during and after the 1944 election. It was a lingering question. Major C.H. Douglas, the British founder of Social Credit, and many of his followers suggested there was a relationship between what they described as an international banking monopoly and the fact that a number of Jewish families were involved in banking. Manning recalled that such conspiracy theories had been around long before the invention of Social Credit

— having been advocated at the beginning of the century by no less than automobile pioneer Henry Ford.

For Manning, though, the task was to see that Socreds who held anti-Semitic views were not in a position to communicate that such views were party policy. One way to do that was to point out that all parties had anti-Semites — or, for that matter, "anti-Catholic or anti-something" members. But Manning felt he had to go further. In due course, he saw to it that the Social Credit Board was disbanded and that the influence of Douglas in the party was reduced. And he maintained consistently that the Jewish community in Alberta strongly supported his government and "would just laugh at this stuff. They knew that it was propaganda in the press."

There was no question, though, that Manning's emphasis early in his premiership was on both monetary and fiscal policy. He undertook a speaking tour in eastern Canada shortly after the 1944 election to explain Social Credit and to talk about what could be done after World War II to see that the Depression did not recur.

By 1945, Manning was trying to rebuild the Alberta economy — and it was working. That meant he could realistically begin to pay down the provincial debt. Aberhart had ignored it — partly out of necessity (there was no money around after the Depression) and partly because of his attitude toward international financiers.

Manning was anxious to restore Alberta's credit rating and to create a better climate for investors. To those ends, in 1945 he formed a joint debt-reorganization committee with the Alberta bondholders. The process was successfully concluded, and the outcome of the experience was to move toward a pay-as-you-go policy. Surpluses, rather than annual deficits, became the order of the day.

In the archival interviews, Manning recalled dealing with American investment houses, represented by Wood Gundy and First Boston Corporation. He was particularly concerned that the negotiated settlement come in under the cap set up by the legislature:

I remember, in New York, going down into a vault under the streets of Manhattan. First Boston passed these $160 million cheques around the table. The plan provided for a serialization of the debt, with the first maturities in three years and the longest [in] thirty. The average interest — the lowest in Canada — was 3.5 percent.

This was a voluntary repayment. But, in the legislature, we had capped the intended total cost at $160 million.

When the figures came in, there in New York, the final total was $10,300 above the ceiling. I asked the First Boston chairman, who we got to know quite well, for a private chat away from the group — about fifteen in total.

I told him: "This is a good deal, we are happy with it. But I want you to understand: we have been living with this out there for ten years. We have gone through an awful lot of hassle over it."

Whatever we did, we would be happy to pay the $10,300 and forget it. But I told him that if I could go back to our legislature and say we did it within the ceiling, psychologically that would be better than saying we could not quite do it.

He grinned and said, "I agree. We'll knock it out of our commission." He wrote the figure down to a few dollars under the ceiling, and we went back in and closed the deal.

Fortunately, those people were all top negotiators. That was their work, and we tried to be the same. And we developed a good rapport with them. They could be tough, but they were sensible, and it was a good relationship.

So it was that the young man who had never formally studied economics or finance, only the Bible and theology, and who had been taught that the international bankers were the enemy turned foes into friends.

Several items of legislation proposed in and around 1946 hinted at the issues Manning was dealing with in bringing Alberta into the postwar era. The Act to Promote Cultural Development grew out of a decision that not enough attention had been paid to arts and culture in a province that, at that point, was a little over forty years old. As Manning notes in the archival interviews, "The emphasis in the early stages was on the economic requirements, breaking up land, getting people settled, providing educational facilities and amenities needed just to carry on." The act was not a big government "throw money at it" approach. Rather, with typical Manning-style prudence, boards were set up across the province to encourage cultural activities. Most of the available money was used for library grants.

The same year, a private member's bill incorporating Prairie Bible Institute of Three Hills was passed. In the run of legislative business, it was not a big thing, but it merits mention because Prairie had an underlying influence on both Alberta and the Mannings. In the archival interviews, Manning notes that Prairie had been incorporated in 1922 under the Religious Societies Land Act, which was usually used to legalize the status of churches. The reason for the 1946 act was that Prairie had grown well beyond being a church — by any definition. It included both the Bible institute and a high school, the latter teaching courses that met the requirements of the provincial secular curriculum.

Under the energetic leadership of L.E. Maxwell, Prairie had grown into an educational complex with worldwide influence within fundamentalist and mainstream evangelical communities. At any given time, it drew one thousand students, more or less, to its spartan campus at the edge of the town of Three Hills.

Maxwell used to advertise that Prairie was training "disciplined soldiers of Jesus Christ." Its graduates, he suggested, would be able to go into the remote corners of the world and face the most rigorous obstacles in order to communicate the gospel. And they would be expected to vow poverty of the kind expected of Catholic priests. True, they would not take chastity pledges, but as long as they were unmarried, Prairie students were expected to keep their minds off sex. And Maxwell ran the school in a way that discouraged thoughts of frivolous romance. Young men and women were not to date or even to walk or eat meals with members of the opposite sex. The rules under which engagements for marriage were to be tolerated were strongly worded and almost as strict.

Prairie was one of several such schools scattered across the prairie provinces. Its chief competitor was Briercrest Bible Institute, just west of Moose Jaw — a place where the rules of romance were not quite as strict. These schools provided a more well-rounded education than secular critics were often willing to admit. Ernest Manning himself encouraged people to look at life, society, and the world with "the Bible in one hand and the newspaper in the other." Bible institute students who acted on that advice found, for example, that religious education courses were helpful in identifying community issues and grasping their significance. And the courses in hermeneutics — biblical interpretation — could prove helpful in understanding and interpreting the law.

Some eighteen years after the passage of the Prairie act, Sandra Beavis graduated from the school with a bachelor's degree in religious education and enrolled in the University of Alberta School of Nursing. Devout, disciplined, energetic, and outgoing, she planned on giving her life to medical missions in some remote country. But one year into her nursing studies, she met Preston Manning. On 23 March 1967, she married him.

The third piece of 1946 legislation that I will discuss was entitled an Act Respecting the Rights of the Citizens of Alberta, sometimes more informally referred to as the Alberta Bill of Rights. It contained provisions regarding credit and credit institutions. Ernest Manning described it as the last major effort the Socreds made to implement Social Credit monetary policy.

During the Aberhart era, there had been acts authorizing the production of what had been known as Alberta Credit and Credit Certificates. The idea had been to circumvent the national banking institutions by providing a form of provincial currency — a way to help ordinary people recover from Depression-forced poverty. Under the proposal, Alberta Credit scrip was to be used within the province for the distribution of goods and services. But the courts had consistently disallowed those acts on constitutional grounds. Now that the war was over and Alberta was beginning to get its fiscal house in order, Manning made one last attempt to legislate Socred-style monetary policies.

The Bill of Rights had two sections, the first itemizing rights and freedoms, and the second providing for a provincial monetary structure. The rights and freedoms were themselves divided into two categories. The first contained the traditional freedoms of religion, association, speech, and so on, all of which created no burden for the provincial treasury. The second enunciated economic rights, and Manning believed that their drafting represented the first time in Canada for such legislation.

It declared that every Alberta "citizen" from age nineteen to sixty was entitled to a job or a social security pension in lieu of a job. Everyone under nineteen had a right to educational and medical benefits as necessary to health and physical well-being. And people reaching age sixty were entitled to pension and medical benefits.

The section on monetary structure proposed a commission that would be responsible to monetize — put a monetary or dollar value on — the productive capacity of the province. And it allowed for the issue of "instruments" — credit certificates — that could be used to transfer that credit from the account of one person to another. Manning always stressed that this was not legal tender, currency, or coinage but a credit transaction. A monetary fund, which would place a dollar value on the productive capacity of the province, would then pay for the economic rights.

But unlike similar Aberhart bills, this act was not to be proclaimed into law unless the courts first approved both parts: the rights and freedoms, and the means to implement them.

In his archival interviews, Manning says that the economic provisions were far ahead of their time — perhaps even excessive. But the government wanted to make the point that people were entitled to economic rights. "I know that's debatable," he speculated.

Both he and his son would become aware of the controversy in later years, as would most fiscal and social conservatives. Economic rights were similar to property rights. Conservatives wanted to see individuals protected constitutionally, while left-leaning people believed it was the state that should be protected. Well, the matter did go to the Supreme Court of Alberta, where it was — almost as expected — ruled ultra vires.

Manning recalled with some amusement an interesting coincidence in the way that the government commented on the court's ruling:

The Alberta Supreme Court chief justice at the time was Horace Harvey, a remarkable man with a mind like a whip, who was active on the bench into his eighties. He was the presiding justice when the arguments were heard, and he wrote the judgement.

In the next legislative session following the court decision, we had a section of the throne speech explaining what the government had tried to do and how it had been thwarted by the court.

The lieutenant-governor (who usually read the throne speech) was ill at the time. So the man who read the throne speech, with the section saying what "my government" thought of the Supreme Court ruling, was the chief justice. I always remember the quaint little smile on his face when he was reading that section!

Manning recalled that some of his own caucus argued that the bill should simply have been proclaimed and then "let somebody stop us."

But I would not agree to that. We had tried that approach half a dozen times before, and we were better to adopt a new strategy altogether.

And we did get a lot of support for the legislation from some rather interesting quarters. The legal profession, for example, was impressed by our referring matters to the courts. We got quite a bit of interest generated and views expressed that the [economic rights] idea was pretty sound.

In Alvin Finkel's *The Social Credit Phenomenon in Alberta* some of the ideological issues that had been part of the 1944 election rhetoric are explored.

Manning never made too fine a point of it, but he and some of his MLAs let it be known that they believed socialism had more of a connection with fascism and Nazism than did Social Credit-style conservatism. At the time, of course, young Canadian men were fighting the Nazis in Europe. Stung by the charges against them with respect to their views on the banking system, the Socreds began to remind Albertans that "Nazi" was short for "National Socialism." As Manning brought his particular stamp to government, he was able to persuade his party that statism and class struggle — not the banking system — were the major opponents to peace, order, and good government.

Another war-related issue that developed during the same period was the Alberta Federation of Labour's pressure to limit the growth of Hutterite and Mennonite farming communities in Alberta. Indeed, the AFL, as well as business groups, were concerned about the negative economic impact stemming from the efficiency of religiously tied megafarms. The AFL argued that such family- and church-based compacts were depriving others — by implication, good WASPs — of jobs. And the business groups, particularly in small towns near Hutterite or Mennonite farm units, were saying that the economies of those towns were threatened because the people in the closed communities would not do business there.

A further accusation was more ominous. Hutterite and Mennonite farmers were accused of increasing their holdings through the fire-sale-price acquisition of farms owned by men who were fighting overseas. Hutterites and Mennonites, as pacifists, did not go to war. So their reluctance to fight was seen as giving them an unfair leg up in farm expansion.

Manning's government somewhat reluctantly developed legislation curbing such expansion — even at the risk of being seen as favouring the established ethnic group (WASPs) over those of Eastern European descent. In effect, the legislation froze the size of the colonies already in existence and prevented the establishment of new colonies any closer than forty miles from existing ones.

There were several facets to the issue, not the least of which was the "not in my backyard" syndrome. Manning noted that most southern Albertans who knew the Hutterites had no objections to them. But they did not want to be surrounded by colonies whose leaders may or may not have been involved in an "encircling" strategy.

Interestingly, Manning recalled that Fred Colborne, the air force representative on the legislative committee dealing with the issue of colony size, came out in favour of the Hutterites on human rights grounds. Colborne was an MLA who had been away from the legislature, fighting, during part of the war. He continued to hold his seat after his return, under a special provision for veteran members. He sat not with the government or official opposition but as an independent member, actually representing his branch of the military.

Colborne submitted a minority report saying that the committee's recommendations were impractical and unjust — and would annihilate the Hutterites. The committee had expected him to speak up for the "boys who had been away, whose land the Hutterites might try to pick up." But he did just the opposite.

Another factor was that the Hutterites had been offered large tracts of good farmland, albeit isolated, in northern Alberta. But the colony leaders maintained they needed the markets of the nearby cities for their products — those markets meant more to them than the community distinctiveness that might grow out of the isolation.

The lawyer for the Hutterites — they retained one even though they were inclined not to go to law — was L.S. Turcotte. In a brief he presented to the legislative committee studying what it described as "the Hutterite Problem," he opined that some Albertans wanted to "deprive this small minority . . . of their right to live in the province."

In the brief, dated 10 February 1947, Turcotte maintains:

> It will be argued that no one is trying to drive the
> Hutterites out of the province, but I say that this is the
> real purpose of the present agitation.
>
> Take the Sunnyside Colony at Warner for example.
> This colony has 4,500 acres of land but only 1,700 are
> cultivated. The rest is rough pasture land. This colony
> has 145 people: In other words, between 11 or 12 acres
> per person. . . . [T]his reminds you of the size of the
> farms in Japan.
>
> Unless the Sunnyside Colony can buy more land,
> they will have to leave the country. If such is the wish
> of the people of this province, then I suggest that the
> Act should say so. It should say that although we
> welcomed these people in 1918 and as late as 1934,
> we, the people of Alberta have changed our minds and
> we now intend to drive them out of this province.
>
> At least let us be honest about it and not bamboozle
> ourselves into believing that we are doing it to help
> veterans get farm lands when such is not the reason
> at all.

Turcotte wraps up his argument by pointing to the Alberta
Bill of Rights, adopted just the year before, which included
equal opportunity for all citizens, freedom of religion and
worship, and the right to engage in any useful occupation.

For its part, the Cardston branch of the Canadian Legion
urged prohibiting the "sale of land to Hutterites or other
communal sects from abroad and who decline to undertake
the duties of citizenship in the fullest meaning. And be it
further resolved that it be made illegal for Hutterites to hold
mortgages or agreements of sale on lands."

Ernest Manning's cautious and pragmatic approach to the
"Hutterite problem" reflected his view that the Christian

should, in biblical terms, be "in the world but not of it." In dealing with the issue, Manning was cognizant of the views of the returning war veterans and the local businesspeople — some of whom were Mormons whose religious devotion was every bit as well honed as that of the Hutterites.

Manning could well understand the Hutterite emphasis on withdrawing from the systems of the outside world. He himself preached that view from his radio pulpit, albeit in a more urbane and polished manner. If he had any advice for the Hutterites, as well as for the Mormons and his own evangelical compatriots, it was that the Christian has dual citizenship. He believed that Christians pledge themselves both to the nation in which they live and to what the Bible describes as "the heavenly city, whose builder and maker is God."

That ambiguity characterized much of Manning's problem-solving approach — and tended to confuse critics, who could not pin him down on whether his faith shaped his politics or vice versa.

In due course, during Peter Lougheed's regime, the restrictions on the colonies were abolished, having outlived their usefulness. And the government of the day's argument was that it violated Hutterite civil rights.

One other event in 1946 highlighting the interplay between Manning's faith and politics was a brief flap over movie censorship raised by Alfred J. Hooke, who held a succession of portfolios over the years in the Socred cabinet.

In the Manning household, as generally prevailed in the evangelical community at the time, moviegoing was not part of the lifestyle. In the churches and Bible schools, the code of behaviour precluded several activities: smoking, drinking, dancing, cardplaying, moviegoing, and swearing. (If Alberta were in the southern United States, the ban would have included swimming in mixed male and female groups, or "mixed bathing," as it was euphemistically described.)

The reasons for disallowing those activities were made fairly clear within the community. Smoking and drinking were bad for the body, which the Bible describes as the "temple of the Holy Spirit." And drinking let down inhibitions and could lead to immoral behaviour. Dancing could lead to sex outside marriage — as could necking (above the neck) and heavy petting (below the neck). Cardplaying could be addictive and thus lead to gambling, which was poor use of the money that God had entrusted to the Christian. Swearing was uncouth and often included using the name of God in a manner for which it was not intended — taking the name of the Lord in vain.

Movies often depicted all the above behaviours in dramatic and graphic fashion. And Hollywood, even then, seemed to want to make the point that sex outside marriage was more common than within it.

In the Manning household, of course, there were many interesting and entertaining activities that made engaging in any of the *verboten* activities unnecessary. Ernest and Muriel Manning had created an intellectually, spiritually, and physically stimulating environment for their two sons. Their dairy farm just outside Edmonton provided a place where the boys could work with the animals. And Mrs. Manning saw it as her task to create a sanctuary for her husband and sons.

But as premier, Manning was also aware that he was managing the province on behalf of all the people, eighty-five out of every one hundred of whom did not hold strictly to evangelical Christian codes of behaviour. And that was the context within which Alfred Hooke's views on movies came into play.

For some years, a former United Church minister and distant relative of Walt Disney, a World War I veteran named Captain Robert Pearson, had been Alberta's film censor. He kept an eye on the contents of these American-made cultural products coming across the border into local movie houses, some of which were located in small towns. In those towns were parents who, no matter what their religious persuasion, wanted to limit outside values. Many of these parents felt safer letting their children go to Sunday school with their evangelical neighbours than to the "picture show." At church, their progeny could learn about the God they themselves had discovered as youngsters in the Catholic or United churches their parents attended.

Not much thought was given, in those typical Alberta homes, to another Hollywood influence — one that had its roots, allegedly, in the Stalinist Soviet Union. True, these parents had heard reports of Communist dictator Josef Stalin's purge of the Ukraine, resulting in a genocide of up to twenty million people. Such reports led them to believe that Stalin was every bit as bad as Adolf Hitler.

Some concerns about the Soviets were rooted in fairly elaborate conspiracy theories. For his part, Ernest Manning was always sceptical of such theories. He thought they were worth a cursory glance and perhaps, in some circumstances, serious investigation. But he tended to take people and movements at face value, expecting that, for the most part, what you saw was what you got. Remember, he liked to turn enemies into friends.

Alfred Hooke was not quite as easygoing about such things. So, when Captain Pearson decided to retire, Hooke, whose portfolio was responsible for movie censorship, decided to hire three people in Pearson's place. And the reason he gave was that much more movie censorship was necessary due to the alleged infiltration of Hollywood by Communists.

Hooke, who held to the old Socred ways until the day he died, was quite convinced that the Soviet Communists were out to take over the world. That many in North America agreed with him was not the point. As the minister in charge of movie censorship, he was sure that part of the takeover would come through control of society's major cultural tools, such as movies.

Manning saw the tripling of the number of movie censors as being related more to the increase in the number of movies, not particularly to a need to keep an eye on their political content. He noted tactfully:

> Practically all movies in those days came out of Hollywood, and there was discussion by organizations and in the press of a concern that Hollywood had been pretty badly infiltrated with, if not Communists, at least with Red sympathizers.
>
> In fairness, I should say that Mr. Hooke was always very sensitive along that line. He was one of the people who were very convinced that Communism was well on its way to taking over the world, and that you couldn't be too careful.

Any understanding of Ernest Manning's views on the influences of Hollywood needs to tie in the previously-stated cultural reality of 1940s evangelicalism in Canada. Most evangelical Christians simply did not go to the "picture shows." Movie houses were part of the world system. That trend began to reverse itself in the 1950s and 1960s. By the time Preston and Sandra Manning's children were teenagers, most evangelicals were as apt to frequent local cinemas as were their more worldly neighbours. And evangelical publications, such as the Billy Graham-backed *Christianity Today*, often included movie reviews and critiques designed to assist their readers in moviegoing choices.

The Alberta premier often took his worldly detached analytical skills to the federal-provincial conferences of the day. And his perspective provided some intriguing insights into what was happening in other parts of Canada.

In his archival interviews, Ernest Manning maintains that tensions between Quebec and the rest of Canada were operative long before the growth of the separatist movement. He recalls Maurice Duplessis, the Quebec "strongman" premier who headed the Union Nationale Party in the 1940s and 1950s. At the time, the gentlemanly Louis St. Laurent was prime minister. As is currently the case, that meant a Quebec-based Liberal prime minister was in power, with the party in power in Quebec City being exclusively provincial. For Manning, himself heading a party that held power in only one province (later in two), the Quebec-federal tensions spilling over into provincial-federal conferences were of more than passing interest.

He notes:

Duplessis would always make an opening statement at these conferences, declaring that he had come to "cooperate and collaborate," but he never agreed to anything. And, quite frequently, he ended up walking out of the conference.

[He] used to give St. Laurent a hard time. Duplessis was a contradictory type; he could be most gracious and charming, but at the same time irritating and sarcastic — if he wanted to be.

Just before one conference, there had been a federal by-election in Quebec, in which St. Laurent's son had run. He had been defeated by a Duplessis candidate. At the conference, Duplessis referred to the defeat every hour on the hour, as proof that Quebec was behind his own position, not that of the federal government.

Then, at the end, he gave a fiery speech and walked out with all his delegation. He returned to Quebec City, where a thousand or more of his people gave him a torchlight parade through the city streets, because he had not "sold out" to the federal government.

I knew him quite well; we used to kid each other around a good bit. Some time later, when we met, he was laughing about the torchlight parade.

He said: "We almost had a foul-up on that one. We had arranged it all before we went to Ottawa. I was to walk out on Wednesday night. Then the conference got behind on the agenda, so I had to phone my boys on Wednesday afternoon and tell them to hold up on the parade until the next night, because I would not be walking out until then."

The point, for Manning, was the organized "spontaneity" of the parade arrangements.

Separatism was never openly talked about in the Duplessis years, Manning said: "Quebec never indicated any intention of getting out of Canada; they just intended to stay and run their own show." Intriguingly, Manning figured that westerners thought more about separation at that time than did Quebeckers: "It was usually over freight rates or similar issues." Quebec's view, he suggested, was that "they were an important part of Canada. If anybody had to separate, it would be the rest of the country, not them."

One of the most frequently repeated assessments of the Ernest Manning government was that it was as close to being scandal free as could be expected, especially considering its longevity. One reason is that Manning had no hesitation in asking for the resignation of any minister whose private activities were seen to be less than arm's-length from his cabinet responsibilities.

The strongest attempt to find the premier himself in a compromising position came in June 1955, during that year's election campaign. Liberal leader J. Harper Prowse accused Manning of trading some of his own farmland for government-owned property on which to drill eight oil wells instead of five. The story was played up by the *Calgary Herald*.

The *Albertan*, the *Herald*'s competition in Calgary, ran Manning's rebuttal on the front page, complete with a full-width head running five inches deep, declaring:

MANNING SHOWS LAND DEAL
CHARGES DON'T FIT THE FACTS
Figures, Dates Cited
Are Mostly Incorrect

The newspaper also carried a front-page editorial saying that, if Prowse was an honourable man, he would apologize.

Essentially, the correct figures and dates corroborated Manning's position that he had made mineral-rights adjustments to his property prior to the 1947 Leduc strike, as had thousands of other Albertans. But the treatment of the story was such that Manning struck hard and fast to ensure that he could retain the trust of the electorate.

As it was, the Socred majority in the 1955 election was cut from fifty-two to thirty-seven, producing the largest opposition since 1940. Immediately following the vote, Manning appointed a royal commission to look into all the allegations. In July 1956, the commission exonerated the government but made some recommendations to tighten management relating to government land purchases.

Seemingly satisfied that the government had instituted most of the restructuring called for by the commission (and the opposition), the Liberal thrust gradually flagged. Prowse left the house in 1958 to return to private law practice. In the 1959 election, sixty-one of the sixty-five seats went to the government.

Preston Manning likes to say that his parents told time by elections. Including the vote in which the Socreds were originally elected, Ernest Manning faced the voters nine times, seven as premier, between 1935 and 1967, the year of his retirement. Each election gave a comfortable majority to the Socreds; in most, the opposition was virtually routed.

Peter Lougheed's Conservatives showed strongly for the first time in the 1967 election, Manning's last. After Harry Strom picked up Manning's mantle, the electorate continued to show signs of slipping toward the Tories. In 1971, the Conservatives took forty-nine seats to the Socred's twenty-five and the NDP's one. Thus began the Tory era, which continues to this day. Two of the premiers, Peter Lougheed and Don Getty, were lawyers and former Edmonton Eskimo football players. Getty's successor, Ralph Klein, is the complete opposite of Ernest Manning in terms of lifestyle. A former radio talk show host, he won his political stripes during his colourful years as Calgary's mayor. He frequently kept in touch with his constituents by holding court in a Calgary watering hole across the street from city hall.

The Tory premiers have never made any attempt to emulate Ernest Manning's faith-politics matrix. But there remains a healthy respect for much of what he stood for. Always, in cabinet, there have been at least one or two ministers whose evangelical faith is a matter of public record. One — a young minister in the Strom government, Ray Speaker — eventually left the Socreds to run for the Tories and served in the Getty and Klein cabinets. While still in provincial politics, he joined Reform, then ran successfully in the 1993 federal election. Speaker, as leader of the Socred club during his student days at the University of Alberta, is thus the lone thread weaving through the provincial Socreds and Tories to Reform.

But the father-son partnership between Ernest and Preston Manning was firming up during the last five years of the father's premiership. It was during the Strom years that they collaborated on *Political Realignment*. And the early 1970s was the period when a Socred-Tory group involving Preston Manning and Joe Clark quietly explored the idea of a merger between the two provincial parties.

CHAPTER 3

The National Pulpit

WHEN ERNEST MANNING made his way to Calgary to enrol
in Calgary Prophetic Bible Institute, he never expected to
go into politics. And he often expressed the view in later
years that such a path was not his first choice. But once the
choice was made, he stuck by it. And while the record shows
that he was a strict adherent of the separation of church and
state, he nevertheless let his faith affect how he did politics.

Later, in chapter 7, we will take an overview of evangelical
Christianity in Alberta as a means to establishing the religious setting in which both Ernest and Preston Manning
have worked. For now, however, we will trace the path that
Ernest Manning trod in translating his faith into the political sphere.

Canada's National Bible Hour, or *Canada's National Back
to the Bible Hour,* as it was known until the early 1970s, began
in 1925 as an outgrowth of William Aberhart's Bible-teaching
activities. In those early years, the Sunday programs would
run as long as five hours. A radio Sunday school for children
began the day's activities, followed by the morning worship
service from Bible Institute Baptist Church, an afternoon
emphasis on preaching from the Bible's prophetic passages,
and an early-evening program featuring gospel hymns.

Ernest Manning began sharing the radio responsibilities in 1930, beginning a sixty-year personal involvement that extends, even today, to the monthly posthumous rebroadcasting of his sermons.

After 1932, the year in which Aberhart was introduced to Social Credit theory, he began mixing political and economic ideas with his preaching. Those political-religious sermons became the catalyst that took him, along with young Manning, into provincial politics.

Once Ernest Manning assumed both the premiership and the full radio responsibilities, the broadcast was reduced to an hour-long format that included all the elements of the five-hour configuration. The heart of every broadcast was the sermon, usually about twenty-five minutes long, including the invitation to his listeners to give their lives to Christ. The radio Sunday school became a correspondence course, geared especially to rural children who could not attend the "real thing."

Muriel Manning, who had been the Calgary Prophetic Bible Institute pianist when she and the future premier had met, took over the NBH's musical side. She formed a small choir that included, for a time, Gordon Beavis, the father of Preston's future wife. The music had a classical touch that grew out of Muriel Manning's conservatory education. The program's long-time violinist was Mary Shortt, well known in Alberta as the first violinist in the Calgary Philharmonic Orchestra. She would often sing hymn duets with Ian Smith, another regarded Calgary musician. In the early days, Mrs. Manning even corralled her husband into a male quartet, known as The Reveille.

When politics took the Mannings to the capital virtually full time, the broadcast site moved from Calgary Prophetic's auditorium to Edmonton's Capitol Theatre and later the Paramount. The irony of using a movie theatre for a service of Christian worship and teaching did not escape the attention of many of the NBH attenders. Indeed, some of them occasionally remarked about the workings of a sovereign God in sanctifying a worldly institution for his honour. After Manning retired from the premiership, the broadcast was reduced to a half hour in length and was done from a studio.

Manning invariably used the expository method of preaching. He would choose a biblical passage and expound it phrase by phrase rather than picking a topic and attaching a Bible verse to it. But the popularity of his preaching in Canada — at its peak exceeding that of Jack Benny's comedic efforts — seemed related to his ability to match current events with his exegetical targets.

When the nation of Israel was formed in 1948, Manning, along with other prophetic preachers, saw that event as the "budding of the fig tree" depicted in Mark 13. He particularly picked out verses 28–29: "Hear a parable of the fig tree; when her branch is yet tender and putteth forth leaves, ye know that the summer is near. So ye, in like manner, when ye shall see these things come to pass, know that it is nigh, even at the doors." While Manning was always careful not to set dates, he consistently suggested that the forming of the state of Israel was one of the precursors to Christ's eventual return.

In a 1980 sermon, Manning suggested that the establishment of Jewish settlements on the occupied West Bank was a continuing fulfilment of that prophecy. That suggestion formed the basis of his theme for the day: "Watch! Watch! Watch!" He maintained that, by the year 2000, life on Earth would be more precarious:

Overcrowding, poverty, and hunger will haunt the globe. There will be more shortages and international tensions. World population will have increased by more that 50 percent to nearly 6.5 billion. Present trends suggest strongly progressive degradation and impoverishment of the earth's natural resource base. Regional water shortages will become more severe as forest destruction reduces the water-holding capacity of the land while demand for water increases. There will be fewer resources to go around, and resource-based inflationary pressures will continue and intensify. There will be increasing potential for international conflict.

Manning often traced many global tensions to Soviet-style communism, indicating that the strategies of Soviet leaders helped to spawn unrest and conflict elsewhere in the world. He seemed not to foresee the breakup of the Soviet empire. Ironically, that took place shortly after he turned the radio program over to Global Outreach Mission.

But it would be an exaggeration to say that Manning's sermons were preoccupied with matters prophetic. Even when talking about the fig tree's budding, he concluded with the strong invitation to the listener to seek Christ as "the rock in a weary land, the shelter in the time of storm."

In a sermon series on biblical figures who enjoyed "unique relationships with God," Manning talked about Moses's successor, Joshua, and his leadership of Israel on the trek to the "promised land." While Manning made no mention of a parallel, experienced Manning watchers may well have read into his comments something of his own pilgrimage — leading Albertans into the promised land after the death of William Aberhart. If Manning did have such a parallel in mind, he did not portray himself as larger than life, however. He simply noted: "God's charge to Joshua made clear that the success of his leadership depended on two things: obedience to the laws of God and a godly courage stemming from an assurance that God was with him and would prosper his leadership as long as he remained obedient." Obedience, courage, and perseverance were the keys to successful Christian service, he insisted.

Manning occasionally picked up a sermon idea from other preachers. One of his last talks, in 1989, entitled "God in Hiding," was drawn from Isaiah 45.15, which reads: "Verily, thou art a God that hidest thyself, O God of Israel, the Saviour." His inspiration for using the text was a Southern Baptist preacher whom he likely heard during one of his winter sojourns to Arizona. Manning was struck by the fact that the text seemed to contradict a central biblical theme — that God reveals himself. The Bible's closing book, Revelation, he said, revealed Jesus Christ as the "eternal Word who was made flesh and dwelt among us and who stressed that he had come to reveal God his Father." But the Isaiah text, he suggested, reiterated two points: (1) God did, at times, hide himself from his people during Old Testament times, and (2) most Christians have experienced at times the uneasy feeling that God was in hiding as far as they were concerned.

Even though Ernest Manning was a layperson, not an ordained minister, he often revealed a pastoral side. This sermon was one such occasion. He suggested that God sometimes hides himself from his people in order to strengthen their faith. Furthermore, he noted, God's adversary, Satan, sometimes blocks their view of God to create in them a sense of divine abandonment. Sometimes, Manning also suggested, the silence of God is intended to provide a magnificent setting for the gospel of his grace:

The revelation of the glorious gospel of grace was God's last word with respect to love and mercy and forgiveness and judgment — limitless love revealed by His sacrifice of His beloved Son; mercy shown by His extending His offer of redemption to all mankind, including His bitterest enemies; forgiveness,

completely without measure; judgment, all borne by
Christ for those who receive Him, and for those who
reject Him, held back while His grace is offered to
the world.

A long sentence it was, but one delivered with a cadence
that his son emulates today in his political speeches. And
the appeal from both men, whether their message is religious or political, is to weigh the options, make a decision,
and stick with your commitment.

In concluding his sermon about the hiding God, Manning noted:

If there is no discernable reason why he seems to
remain silent and in hiding, let us remember and rest
in what he already has told us, "Lo, I am with you
alway, even unto the end of the world." "I will never
leave you nor forsake you." Trust him and like Moses
of old, through faith, "endure as seeing him who is
invisible."

In October 1989, when Manning turned the NBH over to
Global Outreach Mission, he noted that revenues for the
year were just under $300,000, and expenditures about
$36,000 higher. "The shortfall was made up from our
contingency reserve fund," he added simply.

In his transitional announcement, on New Year's Eve of
1990, Manning could not resist leaving listeners with the
sort of strong but kind statement that had marked both his
preaching and political careers:

Perhaps now you can reach for a pad and pencil, and
in a moment I will give you some information about
mailing addresses which you may wish to jot down. . . .
I'll repeat that address so you can check if you have it
right. . . .

Do you know what I would like? I'd like to see them receive a flood of letters from all regions of Canada during this next week, welcoming them to their new broadcast management role and assuring them of your prayers and your support. Will you help make that happen?

There were some characteristics about Ernest Manning's approach to radio pulpitry that assist one in understanding the way he did politics.

At various points along the Christian spectrum, the word "prophetic" is important. But at different points of that spectrum, the word takes on an altered meaning. To the "social gospel" churches (the mainline Protestant denominations and many of the Catholic bishops), speaking "prophetically" means trying to interpret God's view on how human beings should treat each other. Frequently, that interpretation involves advising governments not to take away the social safety net or reduce social spending. Tommy Douglas, along with other early CCF/NDP leaders, bought into that philosophy. Thus, it is not surprising that the United Church and other mainline Protestant denominations have occasionally been referred to as "the NDP at prayer."

In 1951 correspondence to Ernest Manning and other premiers, Fred Poulton of the Canadian Council of Churches pressed for government-subsidized housing. He suggested that lack of adequate housing in Canada was "one of the chief causes of economic and social unrest." In recent years, both the moderator of the United Church and the Canadian Conference of Catholic Bishops have circulated letters to their followers reflecting a similar philosophy.

But it would be unfair to say that socialism has complete control over the social gospel agenda. Douglas and the other social gospel Christians involved in the CCF did have the effect of making that party — and, later, the NDP — a gentler form of socialism than was found in the Soviet Union or Nazi Germany.

Columnist Allan Fotheringham, writing in *Malice in Blunderland*, provides a bit of insight into Tommy Douglas's way of bringing his faith to bear on his political party. Fotheringham says that Douglas was "slightly suspect" with many NDPers because he did not have "that radical urban hatred." "Baptists don't hate — but they don't let down any barriers," Fotheringham noted.

That, then, summarizes the concept of speaking prophetically in the social gospel context. By contrast, the prophetic in the evangelical Christian context involves quite a different approach. And that approach ultimately leads to less government involvement in social affairs and substantially greater input from religious groups. It would, by implication at least, favour a return to the times when churches ran universities, hospitals, and a whole range of social programs.

There are two contrasting ways in which evangelicals speak prophetically.

Ernest Manning's way was to start from the basis that the Bible is God's final authority and that its prophetic books can be used to foresee great trends in history and politics. Charismatic Christians also see prophecy in a way that permits a "word from God" or a prophecy to be uttered in certain circumstances of worship. Manning would have looked a bit askance at such a "word," maintaining that God's written word is the standard by which all spiritual exercise should be measured.

He belonged to a school of prophetic thinking known as "dispensationalism." It was based on the idea of allocating the messages of certain biblical passages to certain ages or dispensations of time. The Plymouth Brethren had originated dispensationalist thinking in the 1800s, and it was popularized in the early twentieth century by Moody Bible Institute in Chicago and by the Scofield Bible. The latter, in the King James text, had study notes compiled by an American theologian, C.I. Scofield. Some western Canadian evangelical wags would occasionally suggest that all a young man needed to be a successful pastor on the Prairies was a set of golf clubs and a Scofield Bible.

One prophetic belief that probably shaped Ernest Manning's political outlook more than anything else grew out of dispensationalism's teaching that the great king of the north in the book of Daniel was Communist Soviet Union.

Manning was not alone in seeing Communism's promotion of atheism, the class struggle, and state control as the antithesis of all that is democratic and Christian. Similar views, articulated in extreme and almost paranoid terms, were part of Joseph McCarthy's American congressional inquiries, in the 1950s, about allegations of the penetration of Communism into the government and society of the United States.

Paranoia seemed to be part of William Aberhart's psychological makeup, but never of Manning's. David R. Elliott and Iris Miller's *Bible Bill*, a biography of Aberhart, in fact suggests that, toward the end of his life, the first Social Credit premier was slipping into a leftist viewpoint that he himself would have denounced earlier. Elliott and Miller suggest that his attempts to control the press, the banks, and other major establishment institutions were rooted in a range of conspiracy theories. And those theories, they claim, helped to define him as a left-wing fascist who was charismatic, skilful in using propaganda, and authoritarian in his view of the state.

The *Bible Bill* authors note with interest that Aberhart was buried not by his Alberta fundamentalist church but by a Vancouver social gospel centre, Canadian Memorial United Church. The officiating minister was Harrison Villett, who had little in common, theologically or ideologically, with Calgary Prophetic. Ministers of Aberhart's own group of churches were apparently unrepresented at the funeral.

Preston Manning says today that, if Aberhart had remained alive, Social Credit would undoubtedly have been defeated in Alberta, because his style and outlook were too combative to take it beyond the point that he did. Aberhart was a pioneer, breaking new ground. Ernest Manning was shaped by a problem-solving and pragmatic mentality. He would move against forces that were disruptive, but he listened carefully to people whose concerns grew out of a range of viewpoints. He was, in fact, a conciliator whose views on reconciliation grew out of his faith.

The 11 January 1961 *Edmonton Free Press* reported fully on Manning's views on Soviet Communism. Manning attacked its rejection of capitalism as well as its promotion of materialism and atheism. And it was on the element of atheism that he concentrated much of his critique. The rejection of God leads to the ignoring of moral and ethical standards and human compassion, he suggested. That stance meant that it was impossible for Communists to negotiate in good faith with people who had religiously based moral constraints.

But Manning never chose to tangle with his neighbouring socialist premier, Tommy Douglas of Saskatchewan, in anything like the way he did with the "king of the north." While he disagreed with Douglas's statist approach to government, he obviously was not prepared to get into a slinging match with him about biblical prophecy. Douglas might have been misguided about the way to use capital and labour, but Manning did not see him as part of the advance of worldwide atheistic Communism. The fact that Douglas never renounced his own teenage Christian rebirth was likely enough to satisfy Manning that he need not see Douglas as an enemy.

Douglas enjoyed referring to Manning as the "Neander-thal Man," — an apparent reference to the latter's adher-ence to tradition. To that, Manning observed amiably that Douglas was "very witty and quick — not very profound."

In the archival interviews, Manning suggested that peo-ple who talked about his "mixing religion and politics" had not quite figured him out. Many who listened to the *National Bible Hour*, he said, entered into a personal spiri-tual experience that would permanently change them. He added:

> If a person's life has been transformed by a spiritual experience, the result . . . will have an impact on whatever they do. I don't care whether they farm, go into politics, or become a doctor or a lawyer. Their analysis of situations, their concepts, their outlook on life, their attitude to other people, are all affected by it. If your Christian experience is real, there is no way you can keep it from affecting your political outlook.

Manning said that, in the early years of Social Credit, critics found it hard to pick up on the real motivation of many of those "Christ-changed" people. The critics only under-stood political motivation in terms of "conniving" and "vote-getting."

> Now, here were people in communities suffering from the Depression, who would say: "Look, we don't want to connive. Here are a bunch of neighbours that have lost their jobs and are losing their farms. We want to help them. We care for them. We care because that's a response of our outlook on life. And here's a vehicle that maybe we can use to do it."

That concept, he suggested, was "utter Greek" to a "secu-lar" politician.

Manning believed that the presence, at the core of Social Credit, of "stable Christian men and women with very firm Christian convictions, perhaps more than anything else, gave stability to the movement." He explained it this way:

> All of us, in what we do that we call service, are motivated by something. Some are motivated by [money], recognition, praise, and acclaim. If they don't get the recognition they think they're entitled to, they get mad and quit.
>
> The ground rule of Christian-motivated service should be love. I know that sounds sentimental. But if that's what motivates us — love for Christ, for what he has done for us, love for our fellows because he cares for them — what difference is it whether you do or don't get dollars?

At that point in his explanation, Manning identified materialism and statism as obstacles to selfless Christian motivation. People who choose materialism over scripture soon see money as their only goal, he suggested. And when fifty cents of their dollar goes to taxes, they want to give up working. The changing motivating factors lead to instability.

> But love [as a motivating factor] is stable. In a family relationship, if some member of the family is in trouble, if there is parental love or love of child for parent that is really deep, sure they may break your heart for a while, but you go on doing the same things because you are concerned.

When the interviewer touched on the role of faith in choosing cabinet colleagues, Manning had this reply:

If I had a choice between two people with comparable qualifications other than the spiritual dimension — experience, knowledge of the area, and so on — and one was a committed Christian and the other was totally uninterested in it, I would take the committed Christian every time.

However, as a pragmatist and conciliator, he had a caveat: "A man can't practice medicine [just] because he is a dedicated Christian. I'd like to see him have seven years at university before he starts carving me up." Obviously, in that instance, Manning's answer took the questioner as far as she had intended to go. A supplementary question could have been raised, however: "What about a Jewish person as a cabinet colleague — or a member of any other non-Christian religion?"

Both Ernest and Preston Manning have been clear that they see religiously based values as better for society than those coming from materialistic or atheistic roots. Thus Ernest Manning's strident rejection of Communism and Marxism, based mainly on their contention that religion is the opiate of the masses.

In emerging into elected political activity, Preston Manning had to contend with something that seldom affected his father. In Ernest Manning's Alberta, those who were politically active came mainly from evangelical, mainstream Protestant, and Mormon backgrounds. There were few Jewish leaders in the pool and even fewer ridings where there were enough voters to choose a Jewish person over someone of some other background.

If Ernest Manning were to have followed the rationale he used in encouraging Mormons into politics, and there is no reason to believe he would not have done so, he would likely have chosen serious and committed Jewish or Moslem people for his cabinet if they had been part of the mix. The anti-Semitic charges against him were generally leftovers of some of Aberhart's more quirky antibank and British Israel doctrines. Manning was able, over time, to rid himself and his party of the fascist tag hung on them by detractors.

In the first eight years of its existence, Preston Manning's Reform Party has faced the same kind of criticism. Some of it has come from the far left. Murray Dobbin, who writes a newsletter called *ReformWatch*, relentlessly paints Reform into a hard-right, fascist, religiously fundamentalist corner. In an article in the left-wing Canadian Centre for Policy Alternatives' *Monitor* of April 1995, Dobbin wrote:

> [Preston] Manning's mentality, rooted as it is in his right-wing fundamentalism, is profoundly anti-democratic. Believing that his end justifies any means, he does not care who joins his party as long as he can control them. This applies to right-wing extremists as much as to genuine democrats. He also welcomes anti-abortionists, death penalty supporters, anti-gun control activists, Quebec bashers and those who oppose immigration from non-white countries — and he controls them all by promising to hold referenda on their issues when he forms the government.
>
> All these extremist groups continue to find a home in the Reform Party. And so do many neo-Nazis, anti-Semites and white supremacists, as long as they do what they're told and don't do or say anything publicly that will embarrass Preston Manning.

Eventually, Dobbin's perspective finds its way into mainstream political campaigning. That happened in October 1996, when a briefing note, faxed from Prime Minister Jean Chrétien's office, coached Liberals to say that Reform is aligned with American extreme right-wingers. Within days, B'nai Brith Canada took the highly unusual step of criticizing the Liberals for characterizing Reform as extreme right. The organization's government-relations director, Rubin Friedman, told Canadian Press: "We find the use of words like Nazi or right-wing extremists, when misapplied, completely dilute and make meaningless, discussions of people who really are neo-Nazis and on the extreme right."

So, the prophetic role that Ernest Manning saw in his preaching had some far-reaching implications. Also endemic to his dispensationalism was the prospect that, at some unknown time, Jesus would return. A sequence of events would follow, eventually resulting in Christ setting up his earthly kingdom. All the Christians of all ages would share in the rulership of that kingdom. The doctrine of the second coming generally has a dual effect on evangelical Christians who take it seriously. It gives them confidence in a sovereign God who, in due course, will work out everything according to his purposes. And it motivates them to serve unselfishly and in dependence on that God, in a way that emulates the actions of Jesus, who has become their saviour.

I noted earlier that it was not the prophetic teaching of William Aberhart that broke through into the depths of Ernest Manning's spiritual being; it was, rather, the preacher's impassioned plea to give his life to Christ. And as he matured, Manning seemed to give increasing emphasis in his Christian thinking to the goodness and grace of God and less to matters prophetic.

Preston Manning moved even further into that area, particularly emphasizing the role of relationships in Christian living. As Reform began to grow, Preston sensed an increasing need to write about where the movement had come from and where he hoped it would head. I recall sitting in on a Calgary meeting of Reform's executive council in 1990. During the meeting, Preston expressed this need to the group and his desire to free himself from regular Reform duties for a few weeks to tackle the task.

Some council members were sceptical about the idea. They pressed him to keep hands on, noting that Reform was at a critical juncture in its growth. Preston went ahead and wrote the book, including a chapter that focused on his spiritual pilgrimage, entitled "The Spiritual Dimension." The book, entitled *The New Canada* and published by Macmillan Canada, became a Canadian best-seller.

The "spiritual" chapter was strong and moving. And it articulated the movement in Preston's life into a faith that was clearly integrated with whatever else he was doing. Thereafter, whenever he was asked in meetings or on talk shows about church and state or his Christian stance, he would talk about it for just a moment and then suggest that the listener "read the book — especially the spiritual dimension chapter."

Of course, one important difference between the father and the son was that the father was able to talk his faith every week for sixty years — and is still doing it on replay. The son had one chance, because he entered politics in an era when preaching on Sunday and governing the other six days had become politically incorrect. That one chance was the book. And when he wrote that chapter, he was deep in prayer about it. The words were carefully chosen, and he believes that he could not have written as he did if God had not been helping him.

The goodness and grace of God is a theme that grew slowly and surely in the hearts of both father and son. The hymnology of the *National Bible Hour* — and, indeed, even of Social Credit — has demonstrated that fact. The marching hymn of Social Credit was always "O God, Our Help in Ages Past." A regular theme song on the *National Bible Hour* was a prophetically based hymn entitled "In the Sweet Bye and Bye." The words of its first stanza and chorus are

There's a land that is fairer than day
And by faith we can see it afar
For the Father waits over the way
To prepare us a dwelling place there.

In the sweet bye and bye
We shall meet on that beautiful shore.

(Repeat)

But another hymn sung at Ernest Manning's funeral
spoke much more of God's present action than of that to
come. It reflected something of a theme that C.S. Lewis
popularized in some of the writing that influenced Preston
during his spiritual quest at university. Lewis spoke of
the "hound of heaven," which sought out wanderers and,
extending irresistible grace, drew them home.

All the implications of that grace were expressed in the
funeral hymn. This chapter wraps up with a repetition of its
words. To get the potential for its social impact, the reader
needs to imagine it being sung by 1,200 people crowded
into a Calgary church, focused on the life that lived by its
words.

O Love that will not let me go,
I rest my weary soul on thee;
I give thee back the life I owe,
That in thine ocean depths its flow
May richer, fuller be.

O Light that followest all my way,
I yield my flickering torch to thee;
My heart restores its borrowed ray,
That in thy sunshine's blaze its day
May brighter, fairer be.

O Joy that seekest me through pain,
I cannot close my heart to thee;
I trace the rainbow through the rain,
And feel the promise is not vain
That morn shall tearless be.

O Cross that liftest up my head
I dare not ask to fly from thee;
I lay in dust life's glory dead,
And from the ground there blossoms red
Life that shall endless be.

CHAPTER 4

The Evolution of the Manning Clan

CRITICS OF THE MANNINGS are often mystified at the way both father and son have mixed a commitment to small government and a dislike of statism with an unexpected depth of social conscience. Particularly, those who equate social justice with government intervention find the Manning ambivalence troubling. While their Christian commitment has much to do with that conundrum, family means a lot as well. And faith and family find themselves mixed together a good deal.

There are many surface contrasts involving the families of Ernest and Preston Manning. For one, Ernest and Muriel Manning made their dairy farm a sanctuary for themselves and their two sons. There was seldom company there — with the exception of the annual tea for MLAS' spouses. Preston and Sandra Manning's home is different. Sandra Beavis came from a large family whose household was always busy, especially with large numbers of young people who were friends of the children. For Preston, that was a change he enjoyed, and as a couple they set out to

3. The Manning family at home in Edmonton in 1947;
from left, Ernest, Preston, Muriel, and Keith Manning.
(Alberta Government Photo)

achieve the same kind of ambience. Having five children instead of two provided an automatic multiplier effect.

For both Ernest and Preston Manning, though, there was another consideration — a very personal one. It involved Preston's elder brother, Keith, who had been born with cerebral palsy and thus required special care throughout his lifetime.

In his archival interviews, Ernest Manning makes reference to "some rather close personal association" when talking about how to work with people who have what today would be described as "special needs." The discussion began when the interviewer said: "You state that certain social programs should somehow be administered as close to the grass roots as possible. Did your government continue to try to do that? And, if not, why did you move away from it?" After some comments about the relative merits of social programs being handled by provincial or municipal governments, Manning noted:

As we move social services entirely into the hands of senior governments, it is destructive to social services.

History shows that where social services are administered and at least in part financed at the local level, there is a fair degree of voluntary supplementary services. People know they are paying for it — and they know the people, so they are interested in them.

There has been so much good done in the past by auxiliaries of different organizations — churches, service clubs, and so on — without a single dollar cost to the public purse. But once these services are taken over by senior governments, that seems to put an end to it. People say: "It is far removed from us. The government is paying for it, so why are we fussing?"

Public volunteer service is people doing it voluntarily because they are interested in people.

It is their neighbour. [Although Manning does not say so, the image of Jesus answering the question "Who is my neighbour?" with the parable about the Good Samaritan was likely in his mind. In that parable, Jesus told of the good person from an alien ethnic group who helped someone who had been robbed and left for dead. And his opportunity to help came after a businessman and a religious leader ignored and avoided the man.]

The problem with the bureaucracy is that in many cases it resents voluntary services. I have seen organizations anxious to help, but who are considered nuisances by those who say there are "professionally trained" people to do the job.

Manning then outlines his views on child care:

There is much to be said for improving the standards of child care. However, we have all seen many mothers who are fond of and love children and have an instinct for what children like. Given a choice, I would want to see my child in a day care centre operated by someone like that, over a trained and skilled social worker who "goes by the book."

And, unfortunately, bureaucratic regulations have often driven out that "instinctive" person. They have no room for a place where some non-professional, non-government-financed group of people say: "Look, we can accommodate a dozen children, and we will take turns looking after them. We will love them from the time we get them until we send them home at night."

The bureaucrat might just respond by saying: "You need four more windows in this room before you can let them in the door . . . and a whole string of other things."

The group with all the love and care to offer says it can't be done. So you lose it. That is sad, and it's a big loss.

Having said all that, Manning warmed to the subject of social policy, particularly the relationship between programs, institutions, and attitudes. He spoke of the Hincks report on mental health facilities, done at the request of then health minister W.W. Cross. Clarence Hincks, who had been head of the Canadian Mental Health Association, looked into issues surrounding conditions at the three major mental health facilities at Red Deer, Oliver, and Ponoka. The Depression had caused a serious falling behind on the upgrading of those facilities, and by the end of the war the catch-up still had not taken place. Hincks recommended the enlargement and improvement of the facilities, proposals that were carried out in due course, but not as quickly as the report urged.

But the nub of Manning's discussion of the question highlighted his "problem-solving, find a balance" approach. Critics who looked for more radical action would have called it the "on the one hand, on the other hand" solution. But for Manning, that was the way to approach it. You had to listen to the various interests, understand where they were coming from, and then take some leadership in solving the problem.

Noting that mental health was a "controversial field," he indicated his preference for the idea that "You treat the overall health of the individual as one situation — whether his or her handicap is mental or physical." In earlier years, he noted, there was a great degree of hopelessness involved in the treatment of the mentally ill, partly because many of the illnesses were lifelong conditions. At the time of the archival interviews, in the early 1980s, he suggested that "things have improved, but we are making many mistakes today, still, because we are still, in a sense, in an experimental period."

The personal experience with Keith came to the surface particularly as Manning spoke of a mentally challenged person's younger years:

> They don't understand why they can't do the things that other children can do. This builds up a terrible amount of frustration on their part. And it leads them to feel rejected by others. The normal child isn't tolerant of someone who can't keep up. They show it by bypassing him. It is not intentional cruelty, but it is cruel.

Manning liked the idea of small institutions: "You get a group of twenty of these kids together — it's almost like a big family." He saw "kind, attentive supervision" as the key to making small institutions such as group homes work. Homes needed to be big enough for peers to share interests and enjoy sports. And he decried the shift to supervision by social workers rather than medical people. A philosophic edge crept into his analysis:

> Over the years, supervision has shifted from medical people to social workers. And no matter how well trained they are, they are not psychiatrists or medical doctors.
>
> This trend goes hand-in-hand with the recent emphasis on "individual rights." One case I am aware of involved a man over twenty-one in an Alberta institution who did not want to take his medication anymore. The supervisors maintained that he had the right not to take his medication. Well, in the old days, when the institution was run by a medical doctor, he wouldn't have that nonsense for five minutes. He

would call the lad in and say, "Look, this is vital to your health. If you don't do this, you are going to have seizures. You are going to be in trouble." And ninety-nine times out of one hundred, he could make the person realize it.

But today, the supervisor will say: "Well, he is over twenty-one, and he has the rights of an adult. What right do we have to tell him he has to take his medicine?"

Manning saw the "individual rights" matter as dangerous in this setting, as he did the issue of "integrating into society" people who had been institutionalized: "There is very little supervision, on the grounds that 'we have no right to interfere.' So people can go off and endanger their lives — without 'interference.' "

That, then, was Ernest Manning's view as the premier in whose cabinet there was a health minister. And that minister, in turn, was responsible for maintaining these institutions, ranging from large hospitals to small group homes. And it was also the view of the father whose elder son needed some of the supervision he was talking about. Critics saw his approach as paternalistic. It was certainly a contrast to his dealings with politicians and voters. As a populist of conservative bent, he never ceased to listen to "the grinding of the axe," no matter the direction from which it came. And he did so to the occasional frustration of his wife, who, to his contention that people needed to be trusted, replied that some of the people with whom he dealt should not be trusted as far as they could be thrown.

It is worth noting that Manning's views on medicare, markedly conservative compared to Tommy Douglas's more socialist approach, moderated through the years. By the time Keith was into adulthood, Manning was ready to have his government participate fully in the federal medicare program that Douglas had prodded into being during his Saskatchewan premiership.

Preston Manning outlines Keith's condition in *The New Canada*:

> The greatest sorrow our family faced during my grow-
> ing up years had to do with . . . Keith. At birth, he had
> been the victim of oxygen deprivation, which had
> destroyed part of his brain. He suffered from epileptic
> seizures, coordination problems and arrested mental
> development all his life until his death in 1986 at age
> forty-seven.

Preston speaks of consultations with Wilder Penfield, the respected Montreal neurologist who pioneered in brain mapping. His recommendations on medication, as well as Keith's enrolment in a special school in upstate New York, brought about a certain sense of normality. On returning to Alberta, Keith lived at first in the Red Deer School Hospital (now known as the Roland Michener Centre, named for the late governor-general who had once repre-sented Red Deer in the House of Commons) and later in a group home and a nursing home in Edmonton. It was at the nursing home that Keith met Marilyn Brownell, who was also a resident of the home: "They decided to marry, and their three years together before he died of a brain tumour were the most contented of his life."

Preston also reveals Keith's faith and their filial relation-ship:

> Besides his reading, the other thing in Keith's life
> was his faith in God. In many respects, his faith was
> childlike, yet it somehow gave a meaning and a purpose
> to his existence which nothing else could do. Most of
> the friends he had — his real friends — were people

he had met at church. It was they who took him to dinner, invited him to their homes, remembered his birthdays, attended his wedding and genuinely grieved at his funeral. Anyone who feels that faith has no role to play in the treatment of the seriously ill and the permanently handicapped — in giving hope and meaning in situations where rationality alone is unable to give hope and meaning — should have met my brother, Keith.

Preston notes that, as a child, he did not understand the emotional and financial strain that Keith's handicap put on his parents. The premier's salary was limited, both his parents' work with the *National Bible Hour* was uncompensated, and his brother's special care in the New York school stretched the family budget to the limit.

With respect to his own relationship with Keith, Preston notes:

> I also suffered from the fear, when we were out together, that Keith would have a seizure. This happened frequently enough to make me apprehensive on every occasion that we went somewhere as a family. When I was younger, I also resented the fact that Keith could not play ball or hockey when I wanted someone to play with. He too resented the fact that he was not physically able to participate in the games and activities in which I took part so easily.
>
> As we both grew older and his condition improved under drug therapy and other treatment, our relationship became less strained. But when people speak to me about the special problems and challenges of living with and caring for the handicapped, I know exactly what they mean. Recognizing that there is still much to be done, I also cannot help but marvel at the

4. Farmhand Preston at thirteen.

enormous progress that has been made since the 1950s and 1960s in recognizing the needs and potential of physically and mentally disabled persons.

In developing Reform, Preston brought a number of faith and family issues and strategies to the table. And woven into them all was that underlying belief in reconciliation.

The home Preston was raised in and the one he and Sandra have made are studies in contrast. Some of the contrasts are generational. His father was a first-generation evangelical and naturally adhered to a stricter, more disciplined approach to family order. And that was easier to accomplish in a setting where there were only two children. But the tendency toward an overly disciplined approach and away from compassion was mitigated by two factors: the Mannings' reconciling faith, and Keith's ever-present mental and physical limitations.

After a few years in the provincial capital, the Mannings acquired a dairy farm within half an hour's drive of The Ledge, on the banks of the North Saskatchewan River. It was in somewhat raw shape when they took it over. Muriel, particularly, wanted to see the homestead turned into a well-landscaped and manicured estate — without spending too much on the project. That meant Ernest, Preston, and Keith were regularly pressed into service on Saturdays to make the place look good. According to Preston, his mother believed that the devil always had work for idle hands to do. Preston recalls the heavy landscaping task of hauling a stoneboat around the yard to water a long row of trees and a fresno for hauling dirt.

Ernest Manning was also very work oriented. Was he a workaholic? Preston does not think so because, he maintains, his father was always in control of his work situation. But the Mannings did believe that work was good therapy and that long hours never killed anyone. The family was involved in dairying as well, but increasingly the farm was run by hired managers, from whom Ernest, Preston, and Keith occasionally took orders. The family saw work and achievement as important family-building elements.

They also believed that the family that prays together stays together. The *National Bible Hour* and Fundamental Baptist Church provided a framework for that prayer discipline. But it was consistently carried out in the home as well. Family devotions, several times a week, after one of the daily meals, were a tradition. A biblical passage was read and discussed, and the members of the family engaged in conversational prayer.

The prayer was generally organized in a way that emphasized

- praise to God for the attributes of the Father, Son, and Holy Spirit;
- thankfulness for the good things in their lives that could be attributed to God's grace, Jesus's intervention in their lives, and the empowerment of the Holy Spirit;
- petitions to God for their personal and family concerns, which might relate to health, the need to get a good mark on an exam, or the stress of conflict within the cabinet;
- intercession for others.

The last element kept the family from becoming ingrown or hardened to the needs of those outside their circle. Because of the wide circle of Christian friends developed through the broadcast, some of that intercession would be for Christians living and working in many parts of the world. The evangelical community has always been very international due to the growth of the missionary movement and the eventual takeover of many of the North American-established churches by national leaders.

Interestingly, intercession also influenced the Mannings' tithing habits. The biblical reference suggesting that "where

5. Preston, at sixteen, with his mother,
on a somewhat formal occasion.

your treasure is, there will your heart be also" played itself out. Indeed, not only did the Mannings never derive income from the broadcast, but they were also financial contributors to it. The rule of thumb was that everything Ernest Manning earned in politics was tithed off the top — before payroll deductions. That meant that ten percent of his annual income, whether from political office or later from company director's fees, went to charitable work of some sort — mostly Christian missions or ministries.

Years later, in 1996, sociologist and World Vision vice-president Don Posterski did a survey that found the most generous contributors to charity were by far evangelical churchgoers. Fiscal conservatism has something to do with that generosity. The churches in which evangelicals — like Posterski and the Mannings — are involved emphasize that it is quite in order for the church to pick up social responsibilities from the government. And the evangelical emphasis is accompanied by a certain amount of "putting their money where their mouth is." Conversely, denominations committed to the social gospel have advocated that government should protect the social safety net, even if it means more taxation and fewer tithes.

But the Mannings have argued that with government funding comes government control and thus an openness to secularization. That, in turn, leads to a socialism that reduces the impact of faith on society.

During his university years, Preston maintained a devotional life that nurtured his quest for a personal faith that was more than simply an inheritance from his parents. His experience contrasted with that of his father's in that he was educated in a secular setting with a range of ideological influences, while his father started off in pursuit of "one book" — the Bible. Preston found that it took his personal devotional life to help him "keep the faith" in the university environment. His reading list was not limited to the Bible;

6. Ernest, Preston, and Muriel Manning disembarking
from a flight at Edmonton International Airport,
1966, during Preston's university years.
(Alberta Government Photo)

85

it included a number of Christian intellectuals who could provide him with university-level credibility for his faith.

In *The New Canada*, Preston talks about that reading list. He starts by noting that someone who was not, by any means, an evangelical believer helped him in his pilgrimage. *Varieties of Religious Experience*, by pragmatist William James, particularly the chapter on "The Right to Believe," provided Manning with the persuasive information that faith was intellectually defensible. His list also includes *Eerdmans' Handbook to the Bible*, Jacques Ellul's *The Politics of God and the Politics of Man*, A.B. Bruce's *The Training of the Twelve*, Fyodor Dostoyevsky's *The Brothers Karamazov*, C.S. Lewis's *Surprised by Joy: The Shape of My Early Life*, and Malcolm Muggeridge's *Chronicles of Wasted Time: The Green Stick* and *A Third Testament*.

Another element in that transition from inherited faith to personal commitment is worth noting — the role of Inter-Varsity Christian Fellowship. Much of Preston's reading list would have been shaped by IVCF, one of whose roles in the university setting was to engender and share an intelligent basis for evangelical Christian faith. Perhaps it could be argued that IVCF did for evangelicalism what the Jesuits, with their emphasis on logic and rhetoric, did for Catholic leadership. IVCF was, in effect, Preston Manning's Christian community when he was at university. Its impact on the lives of future Canadian leaders who grew up evangelical or embraced the faith for the first time in university years is considerable.

A major IVCF influencer was Cathie Nicholls, now in her late eighties. She spent most of her IVCF career in Calgary and Vancouver and was a powerful communicator of an intelligent faith. Through the years, she was like a pastor to thousands of IVCFers. In her retirement, she became a member of the Order of Canada — one of a handful of evangelicals who have been thus honoured.

7. A touch of affection between Ernest and Muriel Manning,
caught by an unknown photographer, in the 1960s.

8. Preston and Sandra's wedding at Fundamental Baptist Church, Edmonton, 23 March 1967. From left, Ernest and Muriel Manning, Preston and Sandra (Beavis) Manning, Mary and Gordon Beavis.

Preston and Sandra's philosophy of the family is not much different than was that of Ernest and Muriel, but it has been applied in a fashion that recognizes some basic facts. First, there were three girls and two boys in the household. Second, the Beavis household had been a noisy, fun-loving place constantly filled with visitors. And that was the kind of home Sandra wanted. So did Preston, in fact. But in many ways, Sandra set the pace around home, just as her mother-in-law had.

In *The New Canada*, Preston speaks amusingly of the effect of his ingrained systems approach to decision-making — and romance:

> Those of us in the management consulting business who are always trying to perfect decision-making mechanisms for our clients and ourselves are usually humbled by the following question. If you ask us how we made the big decisions in our personal lives — where to go to school, what career to pursue, whom to marry, how many children to have, where to live — it is highly unlikely that we used any of the matrix analyses or decision trees or cost-benefit calculations that we are always recommending so highly to our clients. Usually we use our God-given common sense, and the percentage of right decisions seems to be about as high as that obtained by using more sophisticated approaches to decision-making.

Preston and Sandra met when her family began attending Fundamental Baptist Church. Muriel Manning's musical interests helped to create the link between the two families. Muriel had been responsible for years for the musical side of the *National Bible Hour*. In that capacity, she had developed a solid Christian mix of classical and gospel hymns, using a small chorus and a refined blend of organ, piano, and violin instrumentalists. (Today, she raises her eyebrows slightly when she hears about her grandsons' success in bringing Christian rock music into church youth gatherings.) Sandra's father, Gordon Beavis, was a tenor soloist in demand for wedding and choir work. By day, he was a construction company controller who brought the company he worked for back to life through the practice of Christian reconciliation — making some sacrifices of his own in the process. In any case, Muriel recruited Gordon for the broadcast chorus.

In due course, Preston asked Sandra out for dinner on a double-date arrangement with his boyhood pal Ed Wilkins. The couple continued to see each other while she took nursing studies at the University of Alberta. On 23 October 1966, they decided to marry and set plans for the following June, so as not to put too much pressure on her school work. But the next New Year's Eve, after attending a flame-lighting ceremony at The Ledge, they did a little further talking, with the result that the wedding date was fixed at 23 March 1967. Their firstborn, Andrea, arrived the following year. In due course, Avryll, Mary Joy, Nathan, and David came along. (Sandra never did complete her nursing studies. That achievement went to second daughter, Avryll.)

Both Muriel and Sandra Manning are strong women, each of whom decided to support her husband's career. But they have done so in considerably different ways, capitalizing on their own strengths.

A classically trained musician, Muriel Preston was the pianist at Calgary Prophetic Bible Institute when she met her future husband. And through many years she remained the music director of the *National Bible Hour* — a task that involved seeing that both vocal and instrumental musicians were lined up for each program. She was often at Ernest's side through his thirty-three years in provincial politics, at what she figured to be several thousand government or political events.

Muriel Manning spoke out on her own from time to time. In a September 1968 speech to Calgary-area Socred women's auxiliaries, she cautioned against change for the sake of change. On 3 October 1968, she was quoted in the *Edmonton Journal* as suggesting that "we don't grow old [in western Canada] because the country is changing and opening up so fast." And regarding her husband's decision to leave Alberta politics, she told that same *Journal* interviewer: "In addition to our wedding and the birth of our sons, Preston and Keith, the day my husband announced his retirement was the happiest."

Sandra Manning is both cooperative and assertive in her relationship with her husband. She told a group of Christian women in Winnipeg, not long before the 1993 election, that she herself might run for office one day. And in Preston's public rallies during the 1993 campaign, she often introduced him to the crowd.

She has also worked outside the home in recent years to supplement the family income. She sells real estate for Coldwell-Banker in Calgary and has been known to do open houses on Sunday afternoons, after the family attends church in the morning. While she retains the BRE that she earned at Prairie Bible Institute on her business card, the habit of doing business on Sunday reflects the surface changes in evangelical Christianity. In Ernest Manning's time, good evangelicals treated Sunday as a day of rest and worship. In a sense, that was a paradox because, for people who were church leaders, the day was probably the busiest of the week. Commercial activities on the Lord's Day were to be avoided.

Actually, the real estate career was Plan B in the Manning household. Preston and Sandra hoped to persuade Reform to have Sandra set up a "Partners" program for the party caucus in Ottawa. It was a matter of deep concern. For many MPs, particularly those from the west, Parliament Hill is an oppressive and lonely place. The hours are long, and the concentration on matters political is almost obsessive. It has long been known to take its toll on marriages. And with Reform's strong emphasis on the family, Partners seemed to be an essential program. The idea was to have a series of workshops on marriage and the home, particularly geared to those members and their spouses who had to set up two households. But the party saw fit not to spring the funds, and to Preston that was a significant disappointment, because politicians whose homes are stable and supportive are better at their work.

In the summer of 1996, when Preston went on a fact-finding mission to Japan, the party brass did offer to pay Sandra's expenses for the couple to spend a few days in Hawaii before he headed the rest of the way across the ocean. They had hardly seen each other during the previous two months. But the mud hit the fan when a disgruntled Reform ex-employee leaked the information about the minivacation to the media. Tom Flanagan, the former Reform research director who has made it a point to be a friendly critic to the party, said that any contributions he made to the party were certainly not intended for such expenditures.

Not that the party was uninterested in family issues. To the contrary, it has maintained a strong family task force, headed by Port Moody/Coquitlam MP Sharon Hayes. The task force was indirectly inherited from the Conservatives. For several years, the Tories had maintained a "family caucus," some thirty MPs who had encouraged legislation that would support traditional family values. Not coincidentally, family caucus members were mostly Christians of either an evangelical or a conservative Catholic stripe. They had an executive secretary by the name of Greg Pennoyer, a young evangelical Christian who helped them to maintain liaison with organizations such as Focus on the Family.

During the dying months of the Conservative government, Pennoyer became involved in a new group called the Centre for Renewal in Public Policy. Its intention was to advance what looked like a retooling of the Mannings' social conservative thrust of the late 1960s. It wasn't really, but the group did have on board a number of the people who had helped to shape some of Preston's thinking during the years he grappled with the "doing politics Christianly" thing. One member was James Houston, the former Oxford don who had founded Regent College and taught spiritual ethics there. (Regent is the graduate evangelical theological school at the University of British Columbia; Preston sat on Regent's board of governors during the 1980s.) Another CRPP member was Benno Friesen, who served as Surrey-White Rock Tory MP for eighteen years until 1993. Friesen did not much like what he perceived to be Reform's capitalizing on Brian Mulroney's unpopularity. Nevertheless, he was solidly in the same space on social issues as most of the evangelical Reformers.

As a result of the Tories' 1993 shellacking, Pennoyer lost his family caucus job. And CRPP was not ramped up enough to pay him properly, so he took on the executive secretary's role for Reform's family task force, holding down the CRPP and Reform jobs conjointly for several months.

I will wrap up this chapter by talking about the churchgoing decisions made by Preston, Sandra, and their children.

During the years that the children were growing up, their parents made the churchgoing decisions, perhaps with a little consultation with the kids. They left Fundamental Baptist Church as the children started to grow, in part because it was an ageing congregation. For some years, they attended Sturgeon Valley Baptist just down the hill from their miniranch outside St. Albert. Later, they attended Meadowlark Baptist in Edmonton, where a strong youth program attracted their teenagers. Both Sturgeon Valley and Meadowlark are affiliated with the North American Baptist Conference, a mainstream evangelical group that is considerably removed from the fundamentalism of Fundamental.

When the family moved from Edmonton to Calgary in the early 1990s, to be close to Reform headquarters, the children made the churchgoing decision. Their choice was First Alliance, a congregation of 1,500 that is part of the Christian and Missionary Alliance denomination. That group is a tad more conservative than the North American Baptists, but it is also a very proactive denomination noted for innovation in its church-planting and growth strategies.

In the final chapter, as we look toward the future, we will learn more about what the five Manning children are doing in their respective adult and teenage years.

CHAPTER 5

Cultivating the Oil Patch

THE ALBERTA GOVERNMENT had made a pretty fair start on its economic recovery by the time the Leduc oil strike occurred in 1947. But that discovery would make the difference in so many ways

Critics of Ernest Manning have often suggested that he would not have been nearly as popular if oil in abundance had not been discovered. And his friends have replied that God would not have put the oil underground without Manning to exercise stewardship over it.

And "stewardship" was a key word in Manning's mental vocabulary. The evidence indicates that he likely understood that word better than he understood "ownership." That's because his Christian perspective told him, in the words of the Sunday school ditty, that God "owns the cattle on a thousand hills, the wealth in every mine."

Preston Manning was just growing up during the first large surge of oil development. But in his adulthood, the oil patch became important to his consulting work. It shaped him in several ways. Because oil had as much to say about economics and politics as it did about technology, the patch was an underlying influence in his switch, at university, from physics to political economy. Moreover, the opportunity to help Native groups and oil companies to solve problems together, particularly in his years of community development at Slave Lake, was the crucible that turned his ideas of reconciliation from theory to practice.

But it was his father who managed the sweeping changes that oil brought to Alberta. In the next few pages, we will review some of the issues with which Ernest Manning dealt in those years and take a look at some of his thoughts about the way that the "blue-eyed sheik," Peter Lougheed, handled the patch during his premierial tenure in the 1970s and 1980s.

The story of oil in Alberta has often highlighted the tensions between Alberta, the pioneering frontier, and central Canada, the sophisticated consumer and power broker. William Aberhart built much of his profile on continuously attacking the "fifty big shots" who ran Canada from Toronto and environs. And he advanced legislation that bypassed the banks and attempted to control the press, only to find that the financial and information centres in Ontario shot him down, if only by persuading the courts that his legislation was unconstitutional.

When Ernest Manning came to power, the tensions were less a matter of the premier tilting at windmills and more a case of settling down to negotiations. And his aim was to see that central Canada properly compensated Alberta. Instead of castigating unnamed "big shots" in public, Manning tended to stare them down in across-the-table face-offs. Had his faith permitted cardplaying, he would have been a good poker player.

Some of his first pre-oil patch practice came during the war. At that time, the commodity was sugar, and Alberta's competitor was pre-Castro Cuba. Manning was anxious to stimulate industrial development in Alberta so that the province would not remain a "hewer of wood and drawer of water" for central Canada. But he needed capital and war contracts that, without due diligence, would end up in central Canada.

There were three federal wartime agencies with which he had to deal. The first was Munitions and Supply, headed by C.D. Howe, later the Canadian trade czar. In the 1950s, Howe was in the middle of the closure issue that spelled the end of the St. Laurent Liberal regime and brought John Diefenbaker to power. The second was the Wartime Prices Control Board, the bailiwick of Donald Gordon, a bear of a man who later headed CN Rail. And the third was the National Fuel Controller, George Cotterell.

With Munitions and Supply, the trick was to persuade Howe that many of the smaller industries in the west needed the kind of war contracts that would ensure their ability to continue operations in peacetime. As Manning recalls in the archival interviews,

[Munitions and Supply] were reluctant to break the work into small contracts. They were looking for volume and speed — getting the stuff produced so the freighters could haul it overseas as fast as it came off the lines.

It was like the battle that rages today. Ontario and Quebec had the industrial base, so they got the contracts. We got fewer because we had a small base to begin with.

To be fair, we did get some contracts, but not anything significant. However, it illustrated to us that if secondary industry was to develop in western Canada — particularly Alberta — there would have to be capital to get plants operating.

Cuban sugar was a case in point. During the war, Canada obtained most of its sugar from the Caribbean nation. But doing so was risky: without escorts, the sugar boats could be torpedoed by German U-boats.

Meanwhile, sugar beets were a major production item from the well-irrigated fields of southern Alberta. The high sugar content of the beets depended on the sunny climate of the area. Notes Manning:

> We had a couple of sugar factories in southern Alberta, and thought if we could get two or three more, our irrigation projects could be expanded and Alberta could make Canada self-sustaining in sugar.
>
> It made good sense not to pay out foreign exchange to buy sugar in Cuba, then risk having it torpedoed at sea.

Manning also recalls one session in Ottawa with Donald Gordon:

> The argument I used was that if the federal government took the money for every freighter they lost in the Atlantic and applied it to help build some sugar beet factories, the cost would have been the same and Canada would have some permanent assets. And the foreign exchange would have been saved as well.
>
> But it was the old story. They were not amenable to that kind of recklessness out in western Canada. We never did get help on the sugar project.
>
> Donald Gordon and I later became close friends. He was a very capable man. But at the time, he was certainly oriented to the idea that no good thing could come out of Alberta.

Comments about becoming "close friends" with central Canadian luminaries pop up often in the archival interviews. Manning continuously aimed to turn potential enemies into friends. And to many of the early Socreds, that approach was almost like a betrayal.

There was already some oil production before the big Leduc strike, and of course the feds wanted it. George Cotterell was in charge of the production and marketing of petroleum products in Canada during the war, and gasoline rationing was thus under his control. Manning's government had to deal with both him and C.D. Howe on these matters. Manning recalls:

> They wanted Alberta oil wells produced at maximum capacity because of the desperate need for petroleum products. We recognized the need, but our oil-producing program was geared to maximum *ultimate* recovery. That necessitated a more modest rate of recovery.
>
> I remember advising Mr. Howe and Mr. Cotterell that if they wanted wells producing beyond the rate for ultimate recovery, then we needed a directive from them — which they could supply under the War Measures Act. And they gave us that directive.

The tension between Alberta and Ottawa over oil pricing and revenue always lurked below the surface, not only during Ernest's tenure but also when Lougheed was premier. I recall a speech by Premier Lougheed at a Canadian Community Newspapers Association convention in Edmonton in 1979 in which he stated that, if the federal government took certain action with respect to oil revenues, Alberta would consider that action a "declaration of war." I turned to my wife with the whispered comment: "Watch the papers tomorrow. Their headlines will say that Lougheed is declaring war — not the other way around." That is exactly what happened.

Other Alberta leaders could be more blunt. At about the same time, Ralph Klein, then the mayor of Calgary, was widely quoted across Canada as saying that, if Ottawa could not come to terms with Alberta on oil pricing, then those "eastern bastards" should be left to "freeze in the dark."

In Manning's time, the debate had only just begun. The archival interviews of the early 1980s provide some interesting glimpses into the turns that the discourse took in the 1950s and 1960s:

> I am amused today when I hear our friends in Ontario are annoyed because Alberta is asking something closer to the world price for their oil. You often hear them saying, "In those days, when you couldn't sell your oil, we bought it and paid more for it than we needed to pay." That simply was not the case!
>
> Western oil stopped at the Ottawa River valley because, if it went beyond, they *would* be paying more. There was a hassle over extending the pipeline to Montreal. That huge consumer market was supplied entirely by cheaper oil, brought in by tanker from Venezuela or the Middle East. The United States was in the same position — their east coast regions could bring in offshore oil cheaper than they could get it from Texas or Oklahoma.

A pipeline to Montreal would have put the Alberta oil price two or three cents a gallon over that of the foreign product.

The feds tried to get Alberta to reduce its royalties enough to put domestic oil into the Montreal market. Manning's stance was "No. We are not going to subsidize the price of oil just to extend our market." There was a further complication. The United States put a quota on foreign oil, which applied to the Canadian product as well as that coming from offshore. When the Manning government appealed to Washington to take more Canadian oil, the Americans told the Albertans, in effect, to cultivate their eastern Canadian market. There was little sympathy in Washington, because it was already protecting Texas and Oklahoma oil markets in the east through the foreign quota. All in all, it was a buyer's market. Alberta's conventional wells were producing at fifty percent of capacity.

But by the 1980s, it had become a seller's market, and the feds thus stepped in to set artificial prices. According to Manning, "Our only alternative was to regulate field production and prorate it to [the] market." That approach was criticized as being "some nice arrangement that the international oil companies wanted, to hold up the price." Manning believed that kind of criticism was cynical and patronizing, growing out of a classic socialist perspective. It was based on the argument that the multinationals were allowed to call the shots.

There were two aspects to the prorating: that associated with engineering and related to conservation of the reserves, and that associated with marketing. The multinationals were not particularly opposed to the engineering aspects because they expected to be around for one hundred years or more. The marketing aspects were another story. As Manning says,

> We prorated because the international companies were in production, refining, and marketing. But the smaller Canadian producers — who were only in production — would have no market at all. The prorating shifted some of the market to the small operators. It was against the multinationals' interests, and they were vehemently opposed.

During the interviews, Manning speaks at some length about the 1954 Act to Incorporate a Gas Pipeline Company to Gather and Transmit Gas with the Province. The interviewer raised the issue of using a private company and private financing to pursue public goals. Manning's response:

> There was getting to be substantial gas production in the province, and the export market was becoming prominent. The federal TransCanada PipeLine project was under way, and there was already some gas going out of the Peace River area to British Columbia. And there were applications for further exports to the United States.
>
> We were concerned as to what would ensure maximum provincial control over the movement of gas within the province. We wanted to afford an opportunity to supply gas to Alberta communities too small to build gas lines from the supply point.
>
> More importantly, under the laws of the time, any pipelines built under federal legislation were an integral part of the national pipeline — in this case, TransCanada PipeLine.
>
> We did not want that because it would interfere with the dual use of the facilities — delivering for export *and* permitting Alberta communities to tap in.

There were three ways to go: have a private-sector competition for pipeline proposals, set up a crown corporation, or establish a publicly traded company by a legislative act rather than simply under the provincial Companies Act. The third option was chosen: "We felt the company directors should represent four segments: the producers, the Alberta utilities companies supplying its communities, the export companies, and the consumers — the latter appointed by government." By setting it up that way, Manning maintained, there was a built-in incentive for the directors to keep operating costs and profits low, in the interests of viability and service. The company was called Alberta Gas Trunk.

The financing was unique. The act authorized the company to issue up to eight million nonvoting shares plus 2,002 voting shares, all at five dollars apiece.

The voting shares were available to four groups: two hundred to Alberta gas utility companies, fifty to the export companies, 1,750 to Alberta producers and processors, and the remaining two to the two cabinet-appointed directors. Some eighty million dollars was initially raised by the nonvoting shares — more than twice what had originally been projected. The government provided some bridge financing.

The financial community was not too enthusiastic in the beginning because the government insisted that the first offerings go to Alberta people before being put on the open market outside the province. Furthermore, with the restrictions, there was concern whether Albertans would even be interested. But with the help of the banks and the Alberta Treasury Branches (the latter the one vestige of early Social Credit experimentation), the word spread throughout the province. And the subscription interest from ordinary Albertans was such that the open market offering never took place.

But there was a problem: how to allocate eighteen million dollars of stock — which had been the original estimate for the capital needed — to people who had written eighty million dollars in certified cheques. So there was a rebate of sixty-two million dollars, arranged on a draw-selection basis.

Many ordinary Albertans did well on their stock as it advanced in value to ten, fifteen, and then twenty-five dollars per share. But that increase signalled a caution to Manning. After all, thousands of Albertans who had likely never owned a share of anything in their lives had bought this stock.

I was pretty concerned that they would get the impression that this was always what happens when you buy stock. After all, they might go and buy something for five dollars and after three months it was only worth thirty cents. But the experience in this one was all in the one [positive] direction.

The look of Alberta Gas Trunk changed when Peter Lougheed came to power. The nonvoting shares became voting. And Manning himself, interestingly, became a director after he left the premiership, representing the export companies. Eventually, the Lougheed administration changed the makeup of the directorate so that it was simply producer and public representation.

Those changes had the endorsement of Manning: "We would have done it sooner or later." But in the beginning, it was a philosophical thing with him:

We wanted the maximum number of people involved . . . to have a chance to get into the ball game. There was a lot of paperwork, sure, in printing so many stock certificates. But a huge number of Alberta people ended up owning Alberta Gas Trunk stock, which otherwise would never have happened.

A similar stock arrangement was put in place at the time Sun Oil established an interest in the Athabaska tar sands. It did not work as well because Sun lost millions in the first few years. It was not until the early 1980s that the project reached the break-even point. Manning said, in fact, that Sun Oil was not too interested in having Alberta people involved in the financing because the company had "all kinds of money." But the government wanted "ordinary Albertans" to have a crack at it, so Sun Oil okayed a small issue, which, again, was oversubscribed. The investors earned interest on the debentures but not much more.

Manning wrapped up the part of the archival interviews on the oil patch by answering some questions about continuing east-west tensions. From the western vantage point, Pierre Trudeau's energy minister, Marc Lalonde, was a man of aristocratic bearing who often appeared arrogant and uncaring toward anything west of the Ottawa-Montreal-Toronto triangle. Manning's interviewer referred to a story by Don Braid, then of the *Edmonton Journal*, written at the time of the interviews. In that story, Braid said that the Liberals' Ontario-Quebec power base dictated against fair treatment to the west. In response, Lalonde took credit for several federal western initiatives, among them BC northeastern coal, Prince Rupert port development, and CN Rail. Manning's response was wry:

Well, I suppose you could say that people who are that pure politically shouldn't even be in office!

I think, to be fair, accusations against the federal government come from all regions of the country — and they are not wholly true. That is, they have an element of truth, but they are exaggerated.

To be quite realistic, no one could say that [the Trudeau Liberal government] is in a true sense a national government. It has vast regions of Canada with no representation at all. That makes it difficult to deal with national issues.

On Lalonde's points, I think the records speak for themselves. The Hansards are full of cases where work, jobs, and grants have gone to ridings where [Liberal] supporters are located. I don't say they haven't done *anything*, but there is certainly the feeling among some MPs (in both western and central Canada) that you get more attention if you are represented by a Liberal member or cabinet minister. But this is one of the faults of all governments.

The interviewer pointed out that Lalonde had told Braid that the federal fiscal measures had put the Alberta oil industry back on its feet in 1974. (At that time, Peter Lougheed was in the early stages of his premiership, while Manning was in the first years of his time as a senator.) Manning noted:

> I know what he is talking about. But it is only half the story.
>
> The oil industry in western Canada went down badly. The oil rigs were heading out by the dozens to the United States. There had been a protracted war between Alberta and Ottawa on oil royalties and taxation. As a result, we were in the absurd position that — in Saskatchewan at least — the total federal and provincial take in taxes and royalties was more than the total revenue of the oil company in each barrel sold. (In Alberta, it was bad, but not as bad as in Saskatchewan.)
>
> But when the companies were pulling out their rigs, both the provincial and federal governments saw they must do something. So they stepped in and improved depletion allowances, adjusted the royalty thing, and — of course — the flow was reversed, and the companies came back.
>
> So, sure, the federal government did that. But all they were doing was correcting a situation which they created in the first place.

Manning asserted that the Trudeau Liberals got much of their information about the impact of federal oil policies from defeated western Liberal candidates. His implication was that others — more representative of the population of the three western oil-producing provinces — could have provided a more realistic assessment if asked. In retrospect, it seems that the "others" Manning was talking about were Peter Lougheed — who, in due course, did draw a line in the sand that had clear constitutional implications — and Senator Manning himself.

Three years after the archival interviews, Brian Mulroney came to power with the help of those western Conservatives whose half-generation forebears had moved from the Socreds to the Tories. But following the initial euphoria over having so many westerners on the government benches for a change, discontent reasserted itself. It peaked in Manitoba, not Alberta, with the decision to give the CF-18 fighter maintenance contract to Montreal rather than Winnipeg.

That move was seen as a direct slap in the face of the federal health minister, Jake Epp, by the eastern Tory establishment. Until then, Epp was considered one of the most powerful of Mulroney's ministers.

There was a relevant sidelight to that saga. Epp was the titular head of the thirty or so evangelical Christians and fellow travellers in the Tory caucus.

He was catching flack from both sides in his role as health minister because he could not devise abortion legislation acceptable to both his fellow evangelicals and the rest of the voters. Mulroney moved him from health to energy, with the hope, perhaps, that putting him in a role that could make a fiscal difference to the west might recapture some Tory popularity. But it was too late.

And Preston Manning was eyeing all these events with increasing interest. By 1986, he seemed to have a plan in the works.

CHAPTER 6

The Practice
of Prudence

IN THIS CHAPTER, I will discuss a selection of letters
contained in the Premier's Papers at the Alberta Provincial
Museum and Archives. The letters are a window into Ernest
Manning's prudent, problem-solving approach. In most
cases, the letters hint at a relationship between the secular
and the sacred which discloses Manning's penchant for
trying to listen both to God and the people.

From time to time, biographers who approach the Mannings from a leftist perspective note that both men have
lacked compassion because they haven't seemed to work
very hard at having government solve social problems. Alvin
Finkel, in *The Social Credit Phenomenon in Alberta*, notes, for
example, that in a reply to a letter writer who wanted help
for a relative who was suffering from cancer, Ernest Manning suggested that the writer contact the Canadian Cancer
Society. Finkel's implication is that Manning is acting on
the belief that some health care matters should be down-
loaded to private charities.

While the Manning government spent heavily on health care facilities once the oil money was flowing nicely, the premier also urged problem-solving through individual and nongovernment initiatives whenever possible. From that perspective, it is intriguing to read his correspondence with a sense that he wrote like he preached. He aimed to encourage and show respect for the person to whom he was writing, to make his own view clear diplomatically, and, if appropriate, to persuade that person of the validity of his argument.

The letters referred to in this chapter represent only a minute proportion of the material in the Premier's Papers. And this correspondence took place when Ernest was in his thirties and forties — when Preston was a lad. The father was two-thirds of the way through his career in politics at the age when the son was just starting his Ottawa stint.

In both his writing and speaking, Ernest Manning carried himself with a dignity, presence, and control that made him seem, at times, larger than life. Peter Lougheed, who was later Alberta's Conservative premier for fifteen years, noted that Manning's visit to the University of Alberta when he himself was a student there was an *occasion*. But Manning could be self-effacing to a fault, and he was capable of some nicely timed dry wit.

25 May 1943: This letter, from Will J. Green, general secretary of the Gideons (the people who put Bibles in hotels, schools, hospitals, and jails), expressed "personal loss" at the passing of William Aberhart. At that time, Manning had not yet assumed the premier's mantle, although he had been filling the role during Aberhart's illness. Green, noting the possibility of "larger responsibility," said that "I pray that if this comes to pass that you may have a sense of divine guidance and help in a place of larger usefulness." And, like many letters to and from Manning, its close was "Yours in His Service" — always a sign of recognition that both the writer and the recipient were committed, above all, to serving the Triune God.

Manning had a long association with the Gideons, though he was not the kind of person who usually joined such a group. It had been set up as an organization for commercial travellers who would act on opportunities to place Bibles in hotels. In due course, it became more like a Christian-based service club. Obviously, the Gideons were happy to have Manning on board. But as we will see later, they were not the only people looking for the opportunity of Christian fellowship with a Canadian premier.

31 May 1944: This letter, from J.R. Mutchmor, secretary of the United Church's evangelism and social service board, informed Manning that "the provinces which have extended the terms of the Wartime Labour Code to all industry [should] be commended." Alberta was apparently in line for such a commendation.

Mutchmor was one of the United Church's most powerful politicians. His influence came in part from his strong commitment to both evangelism and the social gospel. The United Church, during his time of leadership, had the allegiance of several million Canadians and was growing fast. For a while, the denomination was starting one new church a day, and its leaders — Mutchmor among them — often received as much press ink as did many federal cabinet ministers.

22 January 1945: Ernest Manning grew used to receiving flack for making his faith too prominent a part of his work. But this letter, from Wilfred John Murray, alleged that the premier was a hypocrite. "I will not tolerate you in the government unless you serve the Lord. And I will not have you serve Mammon while I am in the Lord's place," Murray said. And he signed the letter with "Your servant in the Lord Jesus Christ." Murray was not specific about what action had turned Manning into a hypocrite.

2 February 1945: This letter, from the Christian Business Men's Committee international secretary Paul B. Fischer, asked Manning about the possibility of having a CBMC conference in Edmonton. Manning's name had been introduced to the Chicago-based organization by John G. Bennett of Vancouver, a CBMC international committee member. Bennett headed a large West Coast construction firm, Bennett and White, at the time.

In his 23 February reply to Fischer, Manning expressed support for the idea of some CBMC activity in Edmonton and said he had told Bennett he would be happy to provide the names of some Edmonton businessmen who might be interested in being involved. Then, in prudent Manning style, he gently added a cautionary note:

> The majority of the men who would be interested in organizing a unit of the CBMC are evangelical-minded Christians who are already actively engaged in Christian work in connection with their own churches or other Christian organizations.
>
> For example, there is an active Gideons organization in Edmonton, to which many of these men give as much time as they can spare. . . . In addition, for several years I have been carrying on in Edmonton an undenominational Christian work which is really a Christian Laymen's Forum.

The forum was a study group that eventually led to the founding of Fundamental Baptist Church, where the premier was a key lay leader and where Preston spent most of his Sundays as a boy.

Manning eventually supplied a list of names that included Socred national organizer Orvis Kennedy, a close confidante both spiritually and politically. (Kennedy is believed to have been one of the few people who called the premier by his first name.) Apart from that list, Manning was giving his American friend a small reminder that Edmonton was not a big city — about 300,000 in those days — and that too much competition between Christian businessmen's groups might dilute the effort.

While the Gideons was a Christian service club with a specific project — distributing Bibles — the CBMC existed mainly for businessmen to introduce their colleagues to Jesus Christ. Informally, both groups were also good networking agents, with members undoubtedly benefiting businesswise from their association with other Christian businesspeople. But the leaders constantly fought the temptation to make business contacts the main order of the day. It was more important, they believed, to win a person to Christ than to make money off him or her.

Both the CBMC and the Gideons continue to function in many Canadian cities. But they have often been outstripped by Full Gospel Businessmen's International (FGBMI), which adds a charismatic element to its evangelical base. And there is usually a network of Bible study, fellowship, and prayer groups in the office towers of Canada's major cities and in the government buildings of the capitals. Such groups do not usually have the charismatic elements associated with FGBMI. Many are organized by Campus Crusade for Christ, most famous these days for the worldwide promotion of *Jesus*, a movie about the life of Christ.

1 March 1945: George Webber, general secretary of the Lord's Day Alliance, sent Manning a copy of the organization's annual report. In doing so, he said, "we are prompted by the conviction that the future of Sunday in Canada is closely-related to the building of a Christian democracy."

In matters relating to commercial activity on Sunday, evangelical Christians have likely changed more in forty years than in any other way. There has been almost complete accommodation to the idea of the open Sunday. Sandra

Manning holds real estate open houses on Sundays, and churches often have Saturday-night services for families who want to keep their Sundays free for recreational activity.

In the 1920s, Eric Liddell (made famous by *Chariots of Fire*), refused to run in the Olympics on Sunday. Today, by contrast, the dozens of born-again major-league ballplayers would not think of skipping Sunday play, but they also believe that it is important to attend baseball chapel just before the game.

18 April 1945: Ernest Manning wrote a warm personal letter to Robert G. LeTourneau, welcoming him to Edmonton the next month. He wanted to assure LeTourneau that "many sincere Christian laymen are praying for the success of your visit in the salvation of souls and the edification of the Saints."

LeTourneau, from Longview, Texas, was the inventor and manufacturer of earthmovers that featured electric motors in each of their giant wheels. In evangelical parlance, "God prospered him," and he returned the favour by donating *ninety percent* of his income to Christian work. He was also very active in the CBMC and spent much of his time speaking at events sponsored by the organization.

Manning's language was typical evangelical talk at the time. Preston would likely have closed the letter by saying: "Many Christian lay people are praying that your visit will result in commitments to Christ and spiritual growth in those who already know him." And he probably would have expressed some curiosity about the systems LeTourneau used to run his earthmover business.

16 June 1944, 20 November 1945: These two letters came from S.J. Grimwood of the Baptist Union of Western Canada's Edmonton-Peace River Association.

The first was addressed directly to Manning, asking for consideration in the event that Alberta Government Telephones was successful in securing a commercial licence for

CKUA (originally the University of Alberta radio station). The requested consideration was for the possibility of Sunday-evening church service broadcasts on the station. Grimwood argued that the packed churches on Invasion Day demonstrated a surprisingly widespread spiritual hunger. And he pointed out that many people were unable to attend church and would be well served by being able to tune in to a service.

The second letter from Grimwood — who was by then chairman of the radio committee of the Baptist Union — was directed to James McCann, the federal war-services minister. It noted the approval of a licence for a French-speaking radio station at St. Boniface, Manitoba, a large francophone enclave in suburban Winnipeg. Grimwood wondered why no applications from French groups had been turned down by the CBC — then the licensing agency as well as national broadcaster — while many others had been rejected. He particularly referred to the fact that the CKUA application had been nixed.

21 December 1945, 24 November 1948: These were two of several letters dealing with Calgary Prophetic Bible Institute's downtown Calgary property. The first came from A.H. Mayland, who owned an adjacent property and was responding positively to a land-swap proposal that would permit the institute to expand. The second was from the First Church of the Nazarene, one of Calgary's largest evangelical congregations at the time. Its pastor, T.E. Martin, had heard rumours that Calgary Prophetic wanted to sell and wondered whether church and school might strike a deal.

The reply was that there was no truth to the rumours. In the 1950s, though, Calgary Prophetic closed, mainly because the Mannings were spending increasing time in Edmonton and because the growth of some other Bible institutes was making it seemingly redundant. Its remaining supporters threw their lot to another emerging Calgary school, notably Berea Bible Institute.

Eventually, First Church did build a commodious structure on another downtown site. And in the 1980s, the congregation made plans for a megachurch, but it got caught in the economic downturn resulting — many Albertans believed — from the National Energy Policy.

17 January 1946: Manning wrote to W.H. Houghton, then president of Moody Bible Institute in Chicago, giving tentative acceptance to a speaking engagement at the school's annual conference. In the evangelical world, such an invitation was almost like a royal summons. Moody could be described as the "mother of all Bible schools," having been started in the late 1800s by shoe salesman-turned-evangelist Dwight L. Moody.

On the matter of Houghton's "kind reference" to an honorarium, Manning said a firm "no." He pointed out that he never accepted remuneration for his Christian work, except for actual expenses. "I count it a privilege as a Christian layman to have some small part in the service of the King of Kings," he added.

11 March 1946, 16 July 1946: The relationship between the two letters is tenuous but worth exploring. E.F. Molnar, chairman pro tem of the Religion and Labour Council, wrote to "His Excellency E. Manning, Prime Minister of the Province of Alberta." Four months later, Manning wrote to Harry Roye, the public relations man for Charles E. Fuller, the California radio evangelist with whom he kept in close contact. Addressing his letter to "Brother Roye," the premier talked about some of the arrangements for Fuller's upcoming visit to Alberta. He then ended with the hope that "Dr. Fuller's visit to western Canada may redound to His Glory and to the salvation of many souls."

Noting that the Calgary General Ministerial Association backed the objectives of the council, Molnar's letter called for "full employment and full production whose benefits will be reaped equally by both management, investors and labor." And he suggested that this objective and others, seemingly rooted in social gospel concepts, "commend themselves to every person and group that recognizes the laws of God and the claims and . . . needs of humanity. We must free 'man' from fears and wants by humanizing our contractual relationships so that the Glory of the Creator might shine from happy and contented human faces!"

Manning always maintained a cautious approach to labour, and he would undoubtedly have carefully read between the lines of Molnar's letter. Along with many evangelical Christians oriented toward a free market system, Manning saw organized labour as a materialistically based substitute for religion. (My own experience, both as a member of two unions at different times and, on one occasion, being opposite union negotiators at a bargaining table, affirms that "substitute" theory.)

Manning, like many evangelicals, called his Christian colleagues "brother" and "sister" when he wanted to convey a spiritual bond; many union members do the same. Manning worshipped in a church; some union groupings are called "chapels."

And some union leaders communicate clearly that they believe church influence interferes with the public interest. Teachers' union leaders, for example, often oppose trends toward private church-supported education. They believe the public interest is best served by keeping the public school system secular, and they thus call for strong church-state separation. Manning believed strongly in church-state separation as well, but he insisted that self-censorship of one's deeply held values would short-change the public interest by withholding something potentially helpful from the whole political process.

The obvious intention of the Molnar letter was to communicate that there was some common ground. Manning's letter to Brother Roye was an affirmation that the world contained many networks — one of which was the evangelical Christian community. And sometimes the networks interlink.

15 March 1948: A letter to R.C. King of Edmonton from the premier is an interesting example of his occasional attempts to explain, from his viewpoint, the difference between left and right. He noted:

> With regard to your enquiry as to the difference between the various social services at present provided by the state and the situation that would prevail under a socialist economy, I would point out that the major difference is that under a socialist economy, all such services are brought under the jurisdiction of the state, whereas under the system that we are endeavoring to operate in this province, these services do not eliminate similar services being provided by individual medical practitioners or institutions.
>
> In other words, under a socialist state, the ultimate end is a state monopoly over all business enterprises and social services, whereas under a free economy, such state services also provided operate side-by-side with similar services available to those desiring them from private practitioners or institutions.

Both father and son have, at times, written very long sentences.

4 February 1949: In an exchange of letters with J.M. Ruthven, a Pentecostal pastor then working in Grand Forks, British Columbia, Manning offered a little business advice.

Ruthven, who later became one of the best known Pentecostal ministers in western Canada, had written to

Manning describing a portable tent trailer for use in church extension. He had used such trailers for some years and was now trying to get the word out to evangelical church leaders to create a market for them. He was ministering in a Doukhobor community and cut cordwood for them, both to earn his way and to fit in with their doctrine of "physical toil." He concluded:

> I need $1,000 to launch this project. I could go on cutting cordwood and perhaps save that amount in time, but I am consumed with desire to see this thing in action for God now! Do you have any advice or suggestion as to any persons I might contact or how I may possibly release $1,000 from the billions tied up in this old world system?

Manning's reply, in part:

> Without being familiar with the details of what you have in mind, it would seem to me that you might perhaps be well advised to consider organizing a small company or association for the purpose of financing a project of this kind. . . . I do . . . wish you well in your efforts to provide much needed facilities for the promulgation of the Gospel, especially in the outlying communities.

30 September 1949: Al Marsh, director of the Oil Industry Safety Service, publishers of *Oil Industry News*, wrote to Manning asking permission to reprint some of his *National Bible Hour* sermons "whereby we could offer a little bit of God to the petroleum industry workers."

24 April 1950, 19 June 1951: These two letters dealt separately with Jehovah's Witnesses and Plymouth Brethren, reported to be suffering persecution at the hands of Roman Catholics in Quebec.

The first letter was a reply to F.E. Algar of the Canadian Protestant League's Edmonton branch, who had referred to news reports that "Christian Brethren ... in Shawinigan Falls, Quebec, have been criminally assaulted, first by abduction and secondly by mob violence, while practising their religious principles and beliefs." (The group in question, known variously as Plymouth Brethren or Christian Brethren, are not to be confused with the Christian Brothers of Mt. Cashel orphanage infamy.) The Canadian Protestant League was a moderately well-respected defender of Protestantism, and by virtue of its task it occasionally questioned certain practices of the Catholic church. In some respects, the league was well ahead of its time in identifying instances of abuse in and by Catholicism.

The Plymouth Brethren is an evangelical group similar to the Baptists but generally led by lay people rather than ordained ministers. Their lay orientation has allowed many members to be well versed in the Bible and active in voluntary preaching, teaching, and social service activity.

These points have produced an affinity with the Mannings, who have viewed themselves as Christian laymen, not clergymen. Furthermore, the Plymouth Brethren were very influential in the Christian Business Men's Committee, the Gideons, Inter-Varsity Christian Fellowship and Regent College. The former two recruited Ernest Manning for service; the latter two had a profound influence on Preston Manning.

In the context of Quebec in the 1950s, both the Jehovah's Witnesses and the Plymouth Brethren were burrs under the Catholic Church's saddle — as well as that of the government of Union Nationale strongman Maurice Duplessis, who made no secret of his reliance on the Catholic hierarchy in Quebec.

At that time, the Catholic leaders were nervous about the future. The Quiet Revolution, which spawned open separatism as well as a mass exodus from the RC Church, was starting to foment. Consequently, any religious group that operated with no accountability to the Catholic hierarchy was viewed askance. And the Plymouth Brethren and Jehovah's Witnesses fell into that category. While they were dissimilar in most of their beliefs, they shared the seemingly suspicious practice of leadership by unordained people.

The letter about the Jehovah's Witnesses relates Manning's approach vis-à-vis that apparently followed in 1950s Quebec. While Manning told a Mrs. Frank DeMaere that he disagreed with the group's theology and its members' apparent reluctance to become Canadian citizens, he thought that outlawing such groups would only serve to make them into martyrs for their cause.

As indicated in chapter 2, Manning's approach was to make friends out of potential enemies. He had a number of reasons — both religious and political — to be at loggerheads with Duplessis, but he chose to form a firm friendship with him.

30 November 1951, 18 March 1952: These letters represented two different approaches to the housing shortages that were endemic during the time of economic expansion and the postwar baby boom.

The secretary for the Canadian Council of Churches, Fred Poulton, wrote the 1951 letter, noting that the council was appealing "to all provincial and municipal authorities to take whatever steps are necessary to have unimproved property, and property devoted to non-essential activities in their communities, converted into recreational centres and low-cost housing areas."

Mrs. M.C. Auclair had a more personal approach. In 1952, she wrote:

If I do not have lodging before the end of the week, I will have to move my things to your place to live with you. You have a nice home to live in, haven't you. If human beings with reasonable souls are worth more than dollars to you, you will see that I get a real home to live in with my boys.

Not only the home but a salary big enough to make all go well.

There was a postscript to the letter: "I must tell you that I do not want to go and live in Calder. If I am sent to Calder against my will, that is dictatorship and we are supposed to live in a democracy here in Alberta." There is no record of a response from Manning.

November 1951–December 1952: The social gospel churches were pressing for better housing, reduced alcohol consumption, and a ban on lotteries and sweepstakes.

As the economic fortunes of the province improved through the effects of the oil patch, the Manning government entered into a number of vigorous capital projects, particularly in health care, recreation, and housing. Housing projects were often federally assisted. And multilevel government help for seniors' housing was enough to get many churches — both evangelical and social gospel — into sponsoring such projects.

Manning used the proddings of the church organizations as a barometer with respect to social needs. While he seldom moved the government into as much direct activity as the more left-leaning groups wanted, he often accomplished considerably more than they expected. He and his ministers were frequently able to nudge the private and nonprofit sectors into action — and to spare the public purse in the process.

In the archival interviews, Manning suggested that, in retrospect, the oil patch might have done with the Athabaska tar sands what the government in effect did in health care. Many hospitals in Alberta were built before they were needed because the money was available and the construction could be paid for in noninflated dollars. In the tar sands, Manning suggested, very expensive extraction sites and processing plants could have been constructed and then mothballed for decades until they were needed. He noted, in fact, that building facilities before they were needed was a different — but equally valid — way of exercising stewardship as that practised later by Tory premier Peter Lougheed. The Heritage Fund was Lougheed's way of putting away oil money for a rainy day.

18 March 1953: Manning replied to a letter from Lieutenant Wrayburn Whitesell, commanding officer of the Pembroke, Ontario, Salvation Army corps, asking for more information on some sermons he had given on the *National Bible Hour.*

One fundamentalist tenet to which Manning held for some time was his strong preference for the King James Version of the Bible. He was particularly critical of the Revised Standard Version. To Whitesell, he wrote that the RSV "Waters down the fundamental doctrines of the Christian faith and eliminates entirely many vital and fundamental passages of Scripture." In due course, his stridency on that subject reduced as other translations of the Bible, incorporating quality evangelical scholarship, were published.

In the next chapter, we will meander through the evangelical community and look at the many elements that helped to shape the Mannings. Following that, our attention will shift away from the father and more toward the son.

CHAPTER 7

The Community
of Faith

ANY ATTEMPT to understand Ernest and Preston Manning's faith and their effect on Canadian politics needs prior recognition that evangelical Christianity is not monolithic. Many past and current critiques of Social Credit and Reform, particularly those coming from the political or philosophical left, oversimplify the impact of evangelical Christianity on those political movements. From a leftist perspective, for example, there is little to distinguish fundamentalists from neo-Nazis or fascists. But between those two groups is a great gulf. Any interaction between the two is carried on by loners working primarily in isolation. There is some evidence that fascists sometimes try to penetrate fundamentalist communities and churches, but they are usually sent packing when their motives are discovered.

Moreover, Preston and Sandra Manning moved from their parents' fundamentalism into mainstream evangelicalism in the early years of their marriage. Preston today describes the move as sociologically — not theologically —

motivated, and he is partly correct. But that move was similar to what happens to the second generation in many evangelical homes. The shift from an inherited faith to one's own invariably results in some differences in outlook between parents and children.

For Preston Manning, that move meant a deliberately greater emphasis on the relational aspects of faith and less on his father's eschatology. Preston's searching of the scriptures led him to consider passages that helped him to develop concepts of conflict resolution. He did not pay as much attention as his father to interpreting the prophetic parts of the Bible.

Describing the Christianity of the Mannings requires setting it in both the Albertan and the Canadian contexts. In the Albertan context, we will look at Ernest Manning's fundamentalism as part of the province's broader religious picture. That picture includes the range of evangelical Christian movements that developed simultaneously with those directly connected with Manning. Furthermore, Mormons, mainstream Protestants, Catholics, and Hutterites were all significant players in the politics-religion mix in Alberta.

The faith activities over which Manning directly presided included Calgary Prophetic Bible Institute, the *National Bible Hour*, the *Radio Sunday School*, and Edmonton's Fundamental Baptist Church.

Manning held to evangelicalism's four basic premises:

1) a reliance on the authority of the Bible;
2) a strong belief in conversion or being "born again";
3) a commitment to share the faith as widely as possible;
4) a belief in Jesus as Lord over every part of the Christian's life.

As evangelicalism has developed and become increasingly accepted worldwide, those four premises have been used by evangelical leaders to define the movement's uniqueness. One of those definitions is known as the Babbington Quadrilateral, which codifies the premises as biblicism, conversionism, activism, and Christocentricism. It is named for the British theologian who wrote it.

The Babbington Quadrilateral was popularized in recent years through the efforts of the late George Rawlyk, a Canadian historian for whom evangelicalism was a specialty. Rawlyk was a Baptist, a Christian socialist who greatly admired Tommy Douglas, and an evangelical who was considered by many of his contemporaries the movement's foremost historian. He did his work from Queen's University, where he was head of the history department. In the spring of 1995, six months before his death as a result of an automobile accident, he staged a symposium at Queen's called Aspects of Canadian Evangelicalism.

Part of the conference research included an Angus Reid survey that drew the conclusion that about one out of every nine Canadians — including a fair number of Roman Catholics — considers him- or herself to be an evangelical Christian. Rawlyk's findings bore out another survey done two years earlier for *Maclean's*. The magazine's survey added an additional perspective, however. It noted that about seven out of every ten Canadians give assent to one of evangelicalism's major tenets: the divinity of Jesus.

Incidentally, one of the papers presented at the Aspects conference came from Darrel Reid, a Rawlyk Ph.D. history grad who was by then research director for the Reform Party. The political banter between the two men proved entertaining if not enlightening to the larger group, especially when they exchanged views on the validity of Tommy Douglas's role in the development of socialized medicine. Reid's paper was on the history of A.B. Simpson, a Canadian who moved south and eventually founded the Christian and Missionary Alliance denomination. By the time of that conference, both Ernest and Preston Manning were members of an Alliance church.

Intriguingly, both the Queen's conference and the survey related to it were funded in large measure by the Pew Charitable Trust, the philanthropic outfall of Sun Oil. It was Sun's patriarch, J. Howard Pew, who, forty years before, through trust established by their common commitment to Jesus Christ, shook hands with Ernest Manning on the banks of the Athabaska River. That handshake marked the beginning of the mammoth task of developing the Athabaska tar sands.

In a sense, Manning "inherited" not only the Alberta premiership from Aberhart but also that previously cited eclectic group of Christian institutions, all of which could be described as belonging to evangelical Christianity's fundamentalist wing. Manning would handle the affairs of the province weekdays at The Ledge, while his weekend time — apart from family activities — was involved in the supervision of those Christian institutions.

William Aberhart's evangelicalism was combative and passionate. Ernest Manning removed a fair amount of the combativeness but kept much of the compassion and warmth. "Emotive" and "prudent" might be the two best words to capture the difference between Aberhart's and Manning's approach to the faith-politics equation.

Manning believed, like Aberhart, that a personal relationship with Jesus Christ was the answer to the deepest human need. And that is what he preached and practised as he presided over the *National Bible Hour*, Calgary Prophetic Bible Institute, Fundamental Baptist Church, and the *Radio Sunday School*.

During the Aberhart years, fundamentalism was a vigorous and sometimes scrappy contender for things religious on the Canadian scene. Its pugilistic aspect grew out of what its leaders viewed as the religious and political drift leftward of the major Canadian Protestant denominations. That drift was reflected most significantly in the formation of the United Church of Canada in 1925 out of the Methodist, Congregational, and two-thirds of the Presbyterian denominations. Fundamentalists saw the United Church, its emphasis on the social gospel, and the proliferation of that emphasis in its seminaries as a threat to undiluted Christian witness in Canada. They saw this drift as "modernism" — an intellectualized attempt to substitute rationalism for the authority of the Bible.

Baptists were clearly divided by the issue. In Toronto, T.T. Shields, the minister of the prestigious Jarvis Street Baptist Church, led the charge against modernism at McMaster University, then controlled by Baptists. In the west, the same struggle took place at Brandon College, where Tommy Douglas trained for the pastoral ministry.

In Alberta, Aberhart was the best known of the Baptists who broke away from the mainstream Baptist Union of Western Canada. He accomplished that fissure through his control of Westbourne Baptist Church. In due course, Westbourne spun off several churches that formed the Gospel Missionary Association.

One of those churches, Fundamental Baptist in Edmonton, was actually formed out of a Bible study in that city's Masonic auditorium. Formed after Aberhart's death, Fundamental was the home church of the Mannings. Throughout its history, it reflected the more prudent, conservative approach of Ernest Manning, rather than the Aberhart bombast. Indeed, Manning's relationships and connections broadened concentrically through the years. He left behind some of the seemingly religious eccentricities of his mentor once he himself was in charge.

A review of correspondence written shortly before and after Aberhart's death shows that his responses to controversial letters, invariably begun with "Dear Sir" or "Dear

Madam," were argumentative and defensive. Manning's replies, on the other hand, were the essence of prudence. Manning would reply positively, thank the writer for expressing his or her views, commend the writer for taking the time to express an opinion, and encourage him or her to keep looking into the issue. If the topic was religious, Manning was careful not to endorse the writer's views, other than to emphasize the importance of developing a personal relationship with God.

It did not take Manning long to distance himself from those aspects of Aberhart's faith-politics mix that didn't square with the more prudent approach he was careful to foster. British Israelism, a popular movement of the 1930s and 1940s that declared Great Britain to be the lost tribe of Israel, was never far below the surface in Aberhart's time. The combination of British Israelism and Social Credit, with its antibank approach, gave the Alberta political scene an anti-Semitic reputation that Manning gradually wiped away. Indeed, after his retirement from the premiership, he raised the ire of some of the old-line Socreds — such as former cabinet minister A.J. Hooke — by accepting a Canadian Imperial Bank of Commerce directorate.

On the religious side, Manning began to build relationships with orthodox evangelicals whose networks stretched well beyond the fundamentalist corridors. Two such groups were the Gideons, famous for their placing of Bibles in hotels, schools, and prisons, and the Christian Business Men's Committee (CBMC). And two individuals with whom he built lasting relationships were Charles E. Fuller and Billy Graham.

Manning was encouraged by long-time Socred organizer Orvis Kennedy to keep in touch with the Gideons. When the organization's Canadian wing held its convention in Edmonton in July 1968, the premier was the keynote speaker. As reported in the *Edmonton Journal*, he spoke of the need for "a genuine spiritual revival." And he reiterated his oft-repeated view that "Beneath and behind almost all human relationship problems lies the fact of man's wrong relationship to his God. If you can correct the relationship to God, you can do more than anything else to correct the other relationships."

Charles E. Fuller was a California Methodist radio evangelist whose hour-long broadcast from the Long Beach Municipal Auditorium attracted millions of listeners during the 1940s and 1950s. His eventual legacy was the development of Fuller Theological Seminary in Pasadena, today one of the largest seminaries in the world with around two thousand students. It has brought more than a little respectability to the evangelical movement in North America by educating ministers who could serve effectively in mainstream Protestant pulpits without losing their evangelical distinctiveness.

But the Fuller-Manning friendship preceded the seminary days. The link was their radio work. Both originated their Sunday-afternoon broadcasts from large auditoriums; that meant they had local audiences drawn from people who had already been to their own churches earlier in the day. For those people, there was an obvious attraction to being part of an event that carried the gospel they adhered to into national arenas — Fuller in the United States, and Manning in Canada.

During Manning's premiership, the *National Bible Hour* did have a national impact. In the House of Commons, both Prime Minister Jean Chrétien and Conservative leader Jean Charest attested to that impact at the time of Manning's death. Charest, particularly, reported that he had

> very fond memories of his voice — something passed on from generation to generation through the magic of radio.

129

My mother was a very devout Catholic. In our home in the kitchen after dinner in the evenings, I remember very well her listening to the radio show of Ernest Manning. I still remember the jingle. I can still remember that voice and the words. She was a very big fan of Mr. Manning, although I should say for his ideas with regard to Christianity and its basic values.

The "jingle" to which Charest referred was the singing of a seldom-used stanza of the national anthem, which contains the words "Lord of the land, make Canada thine own." The rhetoric of the stanza was sometimes misunderstood by people who thought Manning wanted to create a theocracy in Canada — like John Calvin's "city of God." Rather, Manning saw God's possession of a nation as coming one person at a time, as each considered the claims of the Lord Jesus.

Charest continued: "Through my youth, this voice was very familiar in our home in Sherbrooke, Quebec, thousands of miles away from wherever he was speaking. In that respect, his influence has gone beyond the political forum into every area of our lives." It is noteworthy that, when Charest made those comments on 21 March 1996, the political rivalry between him and Preston Manning, compelled by the Conservatives' attempts to reestablish themselves on the national scene, was on the increase. Charest prefaced his tribute to Ernest Manning by noting: "Evidence [of his influence] is that we have today here in the House of Commons his son, the leader of the Reform Party, who has had some success, I am sorry to say for Conservatives in some regard, in his own political career."

Ernest Manning's friendship with Billy Graham went back to the days when the famous evangelist was working with Youth for Christ. It continued even when Graham, in a break with traditional fundamentalism, began letting theological liberals support his big crusades. Classic fundamentalists did not really consider Graham one of their own, and Manning's willingness to do so was just one example of the Alberta premier's increasingly pragmatic approach to his faith. Graham first raised the ire of fundamentalists in the 1950s when he allowed theologically liberal clergy — many of them social gospellers — to support his sixteen-week crusade in New York City's Madison Square Garden. Purist fundamentalists were usually secondary separatists. They rejected theological liberals and repudiated those evangelicals who cooperated with them. In the United States, Jerry Falwell was a classic fundamentalist for many years. It is only in the past decade that he has warmed a little to people like Billy Graham and to evangelicals in camps other than his own. For Ernest Manning, isolated as he was from the centres of American evangelical influence, the issue was not that relevant.

He became active in a movement to try to get Graham to come to Ottawa and other major Canadian cities for a national centennial crusade. Those plans came to naught. Ottawa Christians were not able to mount the kind of unified effort required by the Graham organization until this past year. In years after the centennial, however, Graham held crusades in Toronto, Hamilton, Edmonton, Calgary, Saskatoon, Winnipeg, Vancouver, and Halifax. And in 1990, his brother-in-law, Canadian-born Leighton Ford, filled in for him in Montreal when a health problem prevented him from appearing.

At the time of writing, the nearly octogenarian Graham and his successor-son, Franklin, are making plans for that long-delayed visit to Ottawa. Undoubtedly, Ernest Manning is looking over the parapets of the heavenly city with pleasure at that development and hoping that, at an appropriate time, he will be able to discuss with the elder Graham the outcome of that mission.

That Manning would get involved in such a national strategy for evangelism was fair evidence of his singular efforts to replicate in others the deep teenage commitment to Christ that gave him such a life focus. For he truly believed that, as important as politics were, communicating the Christian gospel had an even greater value. He was fond of saying that spiritual regeneration could accomplish many changes in human nature that legislative action could not. Social programs could keep people from hunger, but they could not make husbands and wives more faithful to each other, he opined. Only making Christ the head of a home could accomplish that. So each Sunday, no matter what his sermon topic, he would take the last moments of the *National Bible Hour* to earnestly entreat each listener to invite Christ into his or her life.

In 1985, Manning provided a long series on what he described as a Christian perspective on human rights, social injustice, pollution, abortion, capital punishment, the arms race, violence, and drug abuse. In the series opener, he identified "the widespread failure to recognize that there is an inseparable relationship between human rights and individual responsibility." He went on to point out how Jesus, as God the son, laid aside his own human rights in order to purchase redemption for humankind at Calvary. His concluding thoughts that Sunday were:

> Oh, my friend, never in all the annals of time has one done so much for so many at such fearful cost to himself. Surely we who have received Him as our personal Saviour and enthroned Him as the sovereign Lord of our lives should be prepared to set our rights aside for the good of others, as He set His aside for us.
>
> Surely, in the light of what He suffered for you, you must agree that He has a right to your gratitude and your love, and to your response to the invitation He

extends to you to open your life to Him and to receive Him as your Saviour and Lord. I urge you to do so, and to do so now.

Manning never took any pay for his religious work. That did not stop the CBC — which, in the 1950s, was still both national broadcaster and regulator — to closely monitor any on-air requests for money. In fact, some ominous warnings were passed on to the agency handling the *National Bible Hour* bookings, cautioning that even modest references to contributions were in contravention of broadcast regulations.

Manning never resorted to the mocking approach of one American Pentecostal radio evangelist of the time, known as Brother Ralph, who often told his audience: "We aren't allowed to ask for money, but we sure need some!" But Manning was not beyond wondering if CBC's problem with religious fundraising was related to the feeling of some of its political masters that the broadcast gave him too much national influence.

Not many years after Ernest Manning became premier, he and his family moved to Edmonton. By that time, he was representing an Edmonton constituency in the legislature. Eventually, they bought a dairy farm near the city on the banks of the North Saskatchewan River.

Their religious life established its own identity as well. Often the radio broadcasts emanated from the Paramount Theatre in Edmonton, rather than from Calgary Prophetic's auditorium. Manning also started a Bible study in the Masonic Hall, and in due course the group formed the base for Fundamental Baptist Church, located on the downtown outskirts.

Manning was the lay leader of the church, not an unusual arrangement in Baptist churches that rely heavily on congregational autonomy. Because he regularly presided over that ominous and mysterious body known as the provincial cabinet, his fellow congregants thought he would find running the church to be a proverbial "piece of cake." It was always made clear to the minister that he need not worry about church administration; his task was to preach the word and "feed the flock." And he certainly was not expected to bring politics into his sermons.

The church never grew large. In fact, for many years worshippers walked down a few steps into the sanctuary because money had not been available to finish the upstairs. Neither was Fundamental marked by the frequent church fights associated with the congregations in which Aberhart was involved. As in government, Manning kept a steady hand, constantly engaged in the task of problem-solving.

* * *

While Ernest Manning's evangelical faith became well known because of his high political profile, several streams of evangelicalism grew in Alberta during his tenure. An overview of the evangelical subculture in Alberta gives us a useful backdrop to some intriguing elements of Social Credit, Reform, and, indeed, Conservative, Liberal, and NDP politics. The Socreds, the Reformers, and the Tories would not have been nearly as strong in western Canada if they had not known how to tap into the need for evangelical Christians in the west to find a place in the political sun.

But not all evangelicals had the political bug. Some believed that political activity for Christians was wrong — that it was tantamount to setting one's spiritual agenda by worldly standards. Others attempted to develop parties that were overtly Christian in nature.

The Christian Heritage Party is one such manifestation. CHP members do not expect to achieve power for a long time (if ever), but they believe that it is important to place

Judeo-Christian values in the public arena. They are, in effect, "reconstructionists." They would replace traditional pluralistic democracy with a theocracy, in which government and judicial institutions adhere directly to biblical laws and principles. Some of their ideas harken back to the teachings of John Calvin, whose concepts of the Protestant Reformation ultimately shaped Dutch and Scottish Christianity. Many political pundits make the mistake of equating reconstructionism with the kind of evangelical influence that has, on some level or another, influenced all of Canada's major political parties at various times.

Evangelicals who get politically involved usually accept the idea of separation of church and state. That does not stop them, however, from letting their deeply held values shape the way they do politics. But evangelicals, for the most part, seek servanthood rather than empowerment. When they go for power in an aggressive manner, they are not reflecting the actions of Jesus, who consistently eschewed power in favour of service.

In *These Evangelical Churches of Ours* (1995), I split evangelicalism into twelve generic sectors. I will use seven of those sectors in the next few pages to present the evangelical mosaic in Alberta.

1. Mainstream Evangelical

This part of evangelicalism is represented by denominations that adhere to the four points in the Babbington Quadrilateral — biblicism, conversionism, activism, and Christocentricism — without too many other distinctives. They would not, for example, insist that the King James Version of the Bible is the only right one for English-speaking people to use. In Alberta, the Christian and Missionary Alliance along with some Baptist groups, the Associated

Gospel, the Evangelical Missionary, and the Evangelical Free Church, are some of the mainstream players. First Alliance Church in Calgary, where Preston and Sandra Manning are members and where Ernest and Muriel Manning also worshipped in recent years, is a mainstream church. So, too, is Centre Street Church in Calgary, a three-thousand-strong megachurch affiliated with the Evangelical Missionary denomination. Andrea Manning and her husband, Howard Kroon, son of a Christian Reformed minister, chose Centre Street as their church home after their recent marriage.

During the senior Manning's prime, those churches would not have reflected the mainstream. But the Alliance grew in Alberta — and in other parts of Canada, most recently in Ontario — through a spiritual and organizational synergy that was attractive to many suburban and small-town Canadians.

The Alliance emphasized a strong overseas missions program that captured the interest of people who wanted to be part of a global influence. And in the 1950s and 1960s, when other churches were closing down their Sunday-evening services, the Alliance was putting extraordinary efforts into making its services appealing, musically stimulating, and family oriented. People who were disillusioned with their own churches would try out the local Alliance tabernacle on a Sunday night, then soon switch their Sunday-morning attendance there.

The Alliance did not, for the most part, engage in trying to be more theologically pure than other Protestant or Catholic churches. Rather, it relied on warmth, friendship, fellowship, good programming, and other positive attributes to build its congregations.

At Calgary's First Alliance, nurture and education are as important as worship. The shaping of the worship service is as much a matter of pedagogy as theology. The singing in the early part of the service is a mixture of contemporary choruses and traditional hymns. A small band — including drums, guitars, and occasionally trumpets — often accompanies piano and electronic organ for congregational singing. The lyrics, often displayed on an overhead screen, extol the righteousness or compassion of God, the love of Jesus, or the transforming power of the Holy Spirit. The songs usually begin with an upbeat number and move, over a ten-minute period, to more contemplative numbers in preparation for the sermon.

Twenty years ago, the singing would have been led by a middle-aged, suited man whose vigorous arm-swinging cajoled the congregation into a hearty performance. Today a cluster of casually dressed male and female worship leaders provides a more laid-back approach.

The pastor's sermon is generally a teaching event. People are encouraged to follow the reading of the biblical texts in their own Bibles, which they have brought with them. The preaching contains practical information and motivation that can be used by the listeners in the home, the community, and the workplace. The material is not overtly political, but it may touch on the sanctity of life, the importance of marriage vows, and the need for integrity in business and political life.

The fellowship is encouraged through a coffee time after the service. The Alliance learned early that people in the older, more formal churches were used to leaving the service quickly without talking to anyone. It taught that worship must lead to a sense of community if faith is to impact the world when the gathering is done and the people are scattered.

Much of what is said about First Alliance is also true at Centre Street. Its exponential growth has come in more recent years, but would have occurred for many of the same reasons.

2. Pentecostal

The Pentecostal Assemblies of Canada, which now have over 200,000 worshippers each Sunday across Canada, have worked more extensively at developing emotion as a legitimate worship tool. Their distinctiveness is an emphasis on the importance of the Holy Spirit. The practice of "speaking in tongues," along with an emphasis on miraculous healing, distinguishes them in evangelicalism. The Mannings were never part of the Pentecostal movement, but they were certainly aware that it was there.

Ron Graham, in his book *God's Dominion*, provides an interesting glimpse of Central Pentecostal Church in Edmonton, a congregation of 1,200 that meets in a pyramid-shaped sanctuary just a few blocks from Fundamental Baptist. Attached to the pyramid is a three-storey building that houses Northwest Bible College. That building represents what has become, for evangelicalism, one of its sustaining features — the Bible college movement.

For the first few years of his adult life, Ernest Manning was steeped in Bible school terminology. But he would have been taught, at the same time, not to take Pentecostals too seriously. True, they are also born-again Christians, but their very emotive form of worship is likely to interfere with orderly spiritual development. But much of the language was the same, so when it came time for Manning to fill the *National Bible Hour* pulpit, he could speak in a way that built a bond with the Pentecostals.

I recall a chance meeting in the 1950s with Eric Martin, the health minister in W.A.C. Bennett's British Columbia Social Credit government. Martin, a non-Pentecostal, old-style (Aberhart) British Israelite Socred chain-smoker who later succumbed to lung cancer, spoke of the "hidden strength" in his Vancouver Centre constituency. It was Broadway Tabernacle, a large Pentecostal church.

The connection was P.A. "Flying Phil" Gaglardi, the flamboyant highways minister who, on the weekends, pastored Calvary Temple in Kamloops, an affiliate of Broadway. And *his* connection was that he was an evangelical radio preacher attracted into politics because Manning's *National Bible Hour* message had reached across the mountains to him.

Manning, out of his relatively sombre approach to the gospel, consistently steered clear of conflict-of-interest situations — so much so that he was reputed to have run the closest thing to a scandal-free administration in Canada's history. But Gaglardi, with his warm, emotional, Pentecostal style, liked to help his friends. During the week, he wanted to be a friend to the whole province, so he built roads with great gusto. On the weekends, the people in his church were his friends. Many of them he had brought to faith, seeing them delivered from alcoholism, family breakup, or other fates worse than death.

When Gaglardi was in full flight during a sermon, he would begin an earnest entreaty to turn to Christ with the phrase "Friend o' mine." Mel Rothenberger, the long-time editor of the *Kamloops News*, wrote a book about Gaglardi, using that phrase as his title and sympathetically enunciating the preacher-politician's homespun philosophy.

The Mannings' evangelicalism is less boisterous and more studied than Pentecostalism, but they are both part of the same family. Perhaps the simplest illustration of the intriguing relationship between Pentecostal religion and Manning political influence is contained in a story entitled "Alberta's Preaching Premier Who Never Loses," run in the 24 August 1963 issue of *Star Weekly Magazine*. Writer Peter Sypnowich rhetorically asked: "What is the Manning magic?" His reply:

I watched the 55-year-old premier in action at his final rally of the June 17 election, a small Saturday-night meeting at Stony Plain, a small town west of Edmonton, where the Social Credit candidate was in trouble because of rural resentment against oil drillers. A local standard-bearer introduced the premier as a man who "speaks with no forked tongue." Then, in his throaty drawl, Manning began a lucid, detailed, historical exposition of federal and provincial legislation governing the rights of access for mineral development. The only other sound in the community hall came from calloused hands slapping at mosquitoes. When it was over, I heard one man say to another: "He sure talks nice."

Down the gravel road from the community hall, a group of Pentecostal evangelists [sic] shouted praises to the Lord between hot gospel songs over a loudspeaker mounted on a shiny new car. I asked the pastor, a young man who came west from Owen Sound three years ago, what he thought of Premier Manning. "He's a fine man, a man with conviction," he said. Patting the Bible under his arm, he added: "He speaks the truth, the Bible truth."

3. Charismatic

The charismatic movement is similar to the Pentecostal denomination but comes from different historical roots, having often developed within traditional denominations, both Protestant and Catholic.

Currently, the most publicized charismatic activity in Canada is popularly dubbed the "Toronto Blessing." Toronto Airport Christian Fellowship has been holding nightly meetings since early 1994 in a converted trade centre near Pearson International Airport. These meetings, which have drawn up to one thousand people a night, many of them from transoceanic chartered flights, result in attenders laughing, making animal noises, and falling to the floor — apparently under the effects of the Holy Spirit.

Globally, the Pentecostal and charismatic movements are the fastest growing elements in evangelical Christianity. Not only are Pentecostal and charismatic churches expanding, but many evangelical churches previously skittish about charismatic manifestations are cautiously letting themselves come under the movements' influences.

For the Mannings, attendance at First Alliance in Calgary means participating in the more moderate forms of charismatic worship. Some congregants, for example, raise their hands during singing or prayer. On a deeper level, an openness to healing services and expectations of the miraculous are present. In the older fundamentalist churches, miracles of healing have been reserved for biblical times. "Signs and wonders" are no longer necessary to validate God's presence in the world — his written word, the Bible, is sufficient.

4. Evangelicals in the Mainline Churches

Close to half of the evangelicals in Canada are worshippers in Roman Catholic or "big five" Protestant churches: Anglican, United, Presbyterian, Lutheran, and mainline Baptist. Renewal movements are present in those denominations, functioning as a call to return to the traditions that evangelicals believe made the church great in the first place. In every major city, some mainline churches are "catchment" parishes for evangelical expression. Many of the Presbyterian congregations in Edmonton and Calgary fill that role.

As for mainstream Baptists, from whom Aberhart broke, the years of reaction against fundamentalism are long in the past. In fact, Baptist Union of Western Canada churches have played a significant role in linking evangelicalism and the social gospel. Howard Bentall, who was pastor of First Baptist, Calgary, during the latter part of Ernest Manning's premierial tenure, noted that both Manning and Tommy Douglas preached at First Baptist during his time there. "And they both drew equally large crowds," Bentall added.

Baptist historian and pastor Walter Ellis, in an essay entitled "Baptists and Radical Politics in Western Canada (1920–1950)," writes of the contrasting applications of Christian teaching exhibited by Manning and Douglas. According to Ellis, Manning, working from a dispensational basis (the belief that Christ would return and right social injustices), was not inclined to use the political process to preempt God's plan, while Douglas, as a social gospeller, believed that the political process — socialism in particular — was indeed God's plan for the correction of social injustice. Each man's theology was shaped in the years following the Depression. Maxine Hancock, a well-known evangelical author and English teacher at the University of Alberta, puts it more simply. A member of the same church as the first-ever Reform MP, Deborah Grey, she suggests: "The difference between Ernest Manning and Tommy Douglas was that Manning believed that God would bring in the millennium; Douglas thought that was the task of the CCF." Incidentally, Hancock's and Grey's congregation was formerly affiliated with the United Church but left that denomination in the late 1980s over the issue of ordaining active homosexuals to the Christian ministry.

That matter brings us back to the point that there are many evangelical Christians in mainline Protestant denominations. And those people are part of the evangelical mosaic. Some church pundits have estimated that there are as many as 200,000 evangelicals in the United Church, and this number makes them, as a body, stronger than most evangelical denominations. Its largest church, three-thousand-member Metropolitan United in London, Ontario, takes an evangelical stance on many issues but remains loyal to the denomination.

Ernest Manning obviously had an opening into many mainstream Protestant homes in Canada through his radio broadcast. In Alberta, many Protestant ministers, trained in the social gospel tradition, opposed him politically, but they knew that members of their congregations were on his side. And Manning built bridges where he could into those communities.

Roy Bell, a former Baptist World Alliance vice-president, has pastored several of western Canada's largest mainline Baptist churches. He recalls being invited by Manning to a meeting at which the possibility of establishing a Christian university in Alberta was discussed. Manning, as might be expected, was not too happy that so many former Christian postsecondary institutions — such as McMaster, Acadia, and Tommy Douglas's alma mater, Brandon — had become secular public universities. At the time, Bell was minister of Strathcona Baptist, just across the river from The Ledge in Edmonton. And he distinctly recalls that the people the premier called together were mainstream Protestants — not fundamentalists, Pentecostals, or Alliance types. Nothing ever came of that meeting. But in the subsequent decades, three Alberta institutions, affiliated respectively with Lutheran, Christian Reformed, and Seventh Day Adventist denominations, have grown into strong university-level schools.

5. Reformed

Presbyterian and Reformed churches both fit into the Reformed family. The former's roots are Scottish, while the latter's are Dutch. The United Church is also a member of the World Council of Reformed Churches because of its Presbyterian element.

Reformed — or Calvinist — Christians draw their belief system from John Calvin, the sixteenth-century Swiss theologian. One of his major tenets was "irresistible grace," a concept explaining that, when God decides to reach out to people, they will not be able to resist his overtures. Classic Calvinists are also inclined to accept the idea of a theocracy — the possibility that God, if he so chooses, can run a nation or society through his people. That concept is the basis for the Christian Heritage Party, a group that some people confuse with the Reform Party.

Christian-based political parties have been part of the European scene for many years. One of the Dutch-based Calvinist denominations, the Christian Reformed Church, is strong in many of Canada's rural areas. And some members of that church were among the initiators of the Christian Heritage Party, which started about the same time as Preston Manning was getting the Reform Party under way in the late 1980s.

There are many evangelical Christians in the Reformed family of churches, which can be seen to fit into the Babbington Quadrilateral. William Aberhart started his Christian pilgrimage as a Presbyterian, a denomination that accepts a somewhat more diluted form of Calvinism than do its Dutch counterparts. When he became interested in dispensationalism, however, he pretty much left traditional Presbyterianism behind. Had Aberhart lived longer, he might have played out a tighter formal link between church and state. Manning was not so inclined.

The emergence of the Christian Heritage Party provides a contemporary contrast to Manning's approach. Christian Heritage supporters have no truck with the populist approach that has been characteristic of both Social Credit and Reform. Some have referred to the Reform concept of submitting moral issues (such as abortion) to referenda as "mobocracy." They would sooner wait until God chooses to put them in office. Preston Manning believes that politicians — Christian or otherwise — have a responsibility to listen to the people.

6. *Holiness*

This group includes the Free Methodist and Church of God denominations — and the Salvation Army. Many evangelicals consider the Salvation Army their "social gospel" outlet. And they are very proud of a group that so clearly evangelizes while so frequently and effectively meeting human need. In recent years, however, the Salvation Army has sometimes been marginalized by governments that are embarrassed by religious implications within programs they fund.

The Sally Anns, of course, will argue that the reason for their efficiency, effectiveness, and compassion is the spiritual discipline that grows out of their Christian faith. In that sense, they run parallel to graduates of Prairie Bible Institute, who were trained to be "disciplined soldiers of Jesus Christ" — able to work effectively wherever they encounter the gospel's enemies.

7. *Ethnic Evangelical*

Churches have always tended to serve one or two homogeneous ethnic groups. Some evangelicals, in recent years, have developed "international churches" consisting of members of perhaps half a dozen or more cultural or ethnic groups.

Conversely, in many Canadian cities, large evangelical churches serving new immigrants — many of them from

China — have sprouted. Theologically, they run parallel to their Caucasian counterparts; sociologically, they organize themselves quite separately. And it usually takes members of such churches a while to get actively involved in mainstream politics. When they do, the Liberals often prove attractive to them because they have usually been in power when the immigrants have moved to Canada. Raymond Chan, a junior Liberal minister from British Columbia, is one such example; he and his family attend a Chinese Mennonite Brethren church.

* * *

In the political sphere, Ernest Manning built good working relationships with religious people with whom he would have differed sharply on theological grounds. Social Credit always had within its ranks a fair number of serious Mormons. Indeed, Mormonism predominated in some parts of southern Alberta. Cardston was the site of what was, for many years, the group's only Canadian temple.

Mormons, or members of the Church of Jesus Christ of Latter Day Saints, are often cleaner living and more family oriented than many evangelical Christians. And they have a well-developed social safety net that sees to it that no member is found wanting. They share with evangelicals a strong respect for both the work ethic and individual enterprise.

Mormons were in Alberta as a result of migration from the American west in the late 1800s and early 1900s. In later years, as the "oil patch" became a significant factor, a number of the people moving from oil centres in Texas — which were often also "Bible belts" — were either evangelical or Mormon.

Both Ernest and Preston Manning learned much from Mormon colleagues about how faith could lead to effective religiously based social programs. And they share the idea that, when the church and other voluntary institutions live up to their responsibilities, the social costs to government are bound to drop dramatically.

But Mormon theology makes them "competitors" with evangelicals. And their teams of missionaries have often considered evangelicals among the best prospects for Mormon membership. Meanwhile, evangelicals, particularly fundamentalists, have considered Mormons cultic. Past polygamous belief and many of the mysteries surrounding the system of temple worship have kept them apart religiously. And because evangelical and Mormon business-people have been reputed to care for their own, it has been mutually assumed that they would discriminate against each other — all things being equal. But that has not stopped them from breaking bread together politically.

This cursory look at evangelicalism is necessary if the Mannings' faith is to be seen in context. In the next few chapters, we will compare and contrast Preston and Ernest Manning as Preston graduates from university, works with his father at consulting and conflict resolution, and eventually lays the groundwork for the Reform Party.

CHAPTER 8

The Father-Son Partnership

PRESTON MANNING never served in the Alberta government, while Ernest Manning never "went federal." But that dual truism leaves out a lot of interesting overlap in the Manning story. While Preston was never an elected MLA in Alberta, he thought, wrote, asked questions, and made proposals about the state of its politics. And whereas Ernest resisted the temptation to run federally for Social Credit, he surprised a number of his former political colleagues by serving thirteen years in the Senate.

It was during the 1960s and 1970s that father and son maintained their greatest influence on each other. Anything that happened politically or religiously in one life was likely to influence the other.

The rapport between Ernest and Preston Manning began to move into high gear after Preston graduated from the University of Alberta in 1964, with a B.A. in economics. He had begun his education in physics, then switched to a focus on political economy in his third year.

Both his initial choice and the timing of his switch were

reflections of his curiosity and technical bent. Slight in frame and bespectacled, Preston had the appearance of a bookworm when he was a young student. He took physics at first because he believed that many of his questions about the nature of the world could be answered. But he found that his curiosity about people — how they act and work together and how life for them could be different and better — was shifting his focus.

At least three factors — perhaps unknown to Preston — helped to prepare him before his university years for a solid and mutually helpful relationship with his father during adulthood.

The first was the walk across the High Level Bridge over the North Saskatchewan River each weekday afternoon from Garneau Public School to wait for his father to drive him home. He would perch himself at a desk in an anteroom connected to the premier's office by a door, which would sometimes be ajar. There, Preston says, he was able to catch snatches of conversations between his father and the groups of people who would come to see him. Ever the listener, Ernest Manning would spend significant time asking questions of his visitors, trying to ensure that he understood what they wanted. And he occasionally told his son, somewhat tongue-in-cheek, that if he also listened carefully he might hear "the grinding of an axe." Preston Manning enjoyed those visits to the office. He sometimes liked to be there at lunch so that he could eat in the cafeteria in the Haultain Building with some of his father's cabinet colleagues.

A second factor was the health of his older brother, Keith, who, as a result of oxygen deprivation at birth, suffered continuously from epileptic seizures, coordination problems, and arrested mental development. Preston felt a special responsibility toward him and, after his death in the 1980s, sensed some considerable emptiness. The experience with

Keith, especially during Preston's younger years, implanted a tenderness toward human suffering that, to this day, interacts intriguingly with his attention to detail and interest in the technical side of life.

The third factor was Preston's involvement in the *National Bible Hour*, even during his high school and university years. This involvement enabled him to regularly stretch his mind in the task of integrating his faith with his worldview. In his late teens, he was asked by his father to prepare a short talk periodically, especially designed to appeal to young people, based on his own understanding of the Bible and its message. As the years passed, he often substituted for his father in the regular talk. And always he pushed himself to explore biblical passages that emphasized the practical, particularly dealing with the role of faith in business and politics. Both Preston and his father knew that a singular emphasis on Bible prophecy would seem remote to some people. And increasingly, as Preston moved from reflecting an inherited faith to one based on his own response to the gospel, he found that his spiritual disciplines stood by him.

Almost like an evolutionary process, the idea of Ernest and Preston Manning going into business together grew as the father retired from the premiership. Ernest was the introducer. Preston would have encountered great difficulty in establishing contact with those he wanted to brainstorm if it had not been for the trust that key people had in the senior Manning.

Preston's approach was, untypically, to keep the lines of communication open to his father and some others in the older generation. Preston did not keep in touch with them all, a point of contention for many in the older Social Credit set who believed that the premier's son was having altogether too much influence on the premier in the later years of his tenure.

A more accurate reflection might be that the father was gently prodding the son to do his own thing — but to check back with him whenever he wanted. Indeed, Preston persisted in putting together little think tanks of his own contemporaries. However, one of the most intriguing of those groups was not completely of his own making. It was a bipartisan cluster drawn from representatives of — but not formally accountable to — his father, on the one hand, and the emerging Tory opposition leader, Peter Lougheed, on the other hand. One of the bright young men on the Conservative side was future prime minister Joe Clark.

Ernest Manning, knowing that he had been at the centre of power in Alberta before the age of thirty-five, now needed to touch base with a new generation. And what he learned, in due course, was that the Social Credit movement, on the cutting edge when Aberhart and he had come to power, was likely to give way to a new political order in the province. And that order, in the mind of Preston Manning, needed to marry the ideas of fiscal conservatism with a social conscience.

In that pursuit, the younger Manning teamed up with Erick Schmidt, Merv Leitch, and Joe Clark. They were known as the "gang of four." Two, Manning and Schmidt, were aligned with the senior Manning's governing party, and the other two were aligned with Peter Lougheed's Tories, who were in opposition at the time. In retrospect, this team provides a strong clue to Preston Manning's mind-set as well as to the process through which Preston went in adapting his father's outlook to his own view of public service.

While political necessity eventually drove Preston Manning and Joe Clark to be adversaries, with all the accompanying rhetoric, Manning continues to regard Clark highly. In fact, he believes that Clark would have made a better prime minister in the long run than either Pierre

Trudeau or Brian Mulroney, Clark's Tory archrival.

That Clark was a fellow westerner — and Albertan — no doubt contributed to a sense of affinity. But that was only part of the picture. Clark would later espouse the concept that Canada is a "community of communities," in essence articulating the west's penchant for wanting its say in the nation. Both Clark and Manning saw the informal Ontario-Quebec consortium as the main blockage to that "unity in diversity" idea.

Clark, of course, went on to identify formally with the federal Tories. In the mid-1970s, he won the leadership, and in 1979 he served a seven-month stint as prime minister in a minority Conservative government. Thereafter, he took second prize, a generally successful, almost distinguished, half a decade as external affairs minister in the Mulroney government. Manning, by contrast, waited — just as his father had — for something to develop federally. In his archival interviews, Ernest Manning prophetically suggested that Preston was looking for a party with which he would be happy.

But at the time the younger Manning and Joe Clark worked together, they were, in fact, cobbling what could be described as a social conservative political movement. They were quietly working at the behest of their respective political leaders, Ernest Manning and Peter Lougheed. And while the movement did not formally coalesce at that time, the seeds had been laid for the development of a western-based, conservative-leaning, populist party.

Before that happened, however, another "cobbling" took place, instigated by Robert Thompson, the Red Deer MP who had been leader of the national Social Credit Party. In the early 1970s, once the dominant John Diefenbaker was out of the Tory leadership, Thompson figuratively "rolled" Social Credit — largely western based — into the federal Conservative Party. That cobbling held together through

Robert Stanfield's, Joe Clark's, and Brian Mulroney's terms of Tory leadership. The rise of Reform and the general western mistrust of Mulroney's leadership eventually led to the disintegration of that social conservative combo.

Preston Manning's conservatism was not particularly rooted in ideology. Like his father, Preston found a strength in prudence that would lead to a conservative approach to problem-solving. Their argument with Tommy Douglas was in his allegiance to statism and class struggle, which they believed to be an unnecessary compromise of the Christian gospel.

Consistently, Preston Manning advocated reconciliation over adversarialism. And in so doing, he stubbornly insisted that, while socialism and the social gospel did not hold the solutions to the human condition, they raised questions for which answers were needed. But it was not only the left that resisted the conciliatory approach. Tom Flanagan, the Reform Party's policy director in its early years, wrote in *Waiting for the Wave* of his misgivings about what he perceived to be the disproportionate number of evangelical Christians around Manning. He wanted to see the party behave in a more purely conservative way.

But Flanagan did not see the conciliatory approach as a tool for populism so much as the practice of what he called "monism." And to him, monism was an attempt to get everybody under one banner — presumably Preston Manning's. Manning's conciliatory approach was deeply rooted, though, in his understanding of the Christian gospel, an understanding that he shared with his father but that he took into new fields of thought.

Neither Manning was inclined to support setting up a Christian political party. For Ernest Manning, defence of that concept was much easier than it was for his son. He and William Aberhart had the influence of the radio program to make an informal tie between Christianity and politics — but its success was based on integrity shown separately in both the religious and the political spheres. His continued strength at the polls allowed Manning to stay in power, to do so with little legislative opposition, and to maintain his integrity. No matter what criticisms were levelled against him, those implying that he was unprincipled or dishonest simply could not stick. And he was able to inform the public that the reason he was both principled and able rested in his commitment to Jesus Christ.

For Preston Manning, the challenge has been a little different. He is in the federal field and in opposition. The prevailing patterns of thought in the rest of Canada are, for him, unfamiliarly diverse. Being in opposition requires him to be adversarial; he cannot practise, in any more than a peripheral way, his deeply held views on reconciliation.

For over forty years, Preston has talked about wanting to "do politics Christianly." It was a code phrase understood by those of his own generation who, like him, had inherited an evangelical faith that, in due course, they needed to make their own. And it was in the early years of the think tanks — specifically in the early 1970s, shortly after his father retired from the Alberta premiership — that Manning chose to use that concept to bring together some of his evangelical contemporaries. Among others, Preston chose Donald Posterski, a young Nazarene church pastor in Edmonton, and Donald Page, a history teacher at the University of Regina. Page recalls that the process was simple enough. Manning would circulate some written comments to the group, asking for their feedback on a subject such as the social relevance of the biblical concept of reconciliation.

By implication, Preston was interested in neither a Christian political party nor a socialist party with Christian influences. But, ever conscious that, in any society, there is a plethora of views, he preferred to use a Christian-based conciliatory process to help people work with each other. He had two reasons for not embracing Christian socialism. First, he did not believe that reconciliation could be "reconciled" with the class struggle; second, he thought that a bureaucracy desirous of maintaining strong state control is a dehumanizing instrument that, in effect, defeats its own purposes.

Preston's choice of Christian braintrusters was most interesting. Both Page and Posterski, like Manning, were second-generation evangelicals, but they were not rebels. To the contrary, they had been taught that they could not receive God's favour on the coattails of their parents' faith. But in coming to faith for themselves, they developed some different perspectives. Their university education made them used to the discipline of having their ideas and values tested by those who differed from them.

And the career paths followed by those with whom Preston chose to brainstorm have been no less intriguing. After his teaching stint in Regina, Page became a senior policy advisor in the external affairs department in Ottawa. He wrote briefing papers and speeches for several cabinet ministers (including Joe Clark) in both Liberal and Conservative governments. While in the capital, Page played a key role in developing the Public Service Christian Fellowship as a place where Parliament Hill staffers could pray and study the Bible together. In the late 1980s, he moved to the West Coast to become academic vice-president of Trinity Western University. In both situations, he actively encouraged an interface between evangelical and secular values. Trinity was constantly misidentified, in the "real world," as a Bible school. Secularists in the media had great difficulty imagining that evangelicals could think rationally and logically. Using both his diplomatic and academic disciplines, Page has done much to create wider acceptance for the university.

Posterski, for his part, headed up Inter-Varsity Christian Fellowship in Ontario before becoming vice-president of national programs for World Vision Canada. In his IVCF role, he was involved in helping students to develop their Christian faith in the university setting. Often, those students were going through the same process that he had — the pilgrimage from inherited to personal faith. And at World Vision, he has been involved in persuading evangelical Christians that government ought not to be totally responsible for the social safety net, that there is an important role for churches and church-related organizations to play, especially when governments are trying to cut costs. In that role, Posterski provides an alternative to the 1990s-style social gospel of the mainline Protestant churches and Catholic bishops that believe that to be prophetic is to tell the government it ought to be more involved — not less — in providing the social safety net.

In his early postuniversity years, much of Preston Manning's work — including the interface with Joe Clark — was done under an organization known as the National Public Affairs Research Foundation. It had been put together with the help of some oil patch money to ensure that there was an arm's length relationship with the governments of the day. Two other projects that Manning carried out under the foundation were the *White Paper on Human Resources Development*, produced for the Alberta government, and the research for the *Political Realignment* book. Today, Manning sees all three projects as having laid the groundwork for the evolution of the Reform Party almost two decades later.

The *White Paper*, written in 1967, was designed to put on record that people who believe in the free market, private ownership of property, and individual enterprise are quite capable of social concern and humanitarianism. It was Preston's first widely circulated opportunity to move conservative-leaning people out of the defensive corners into which they believed socialists and social gospellers often painted them. Thirty years later, when Preston talks about the job-creating effects of deficit reduction followed by lower taxes, he is hammering away at a *White Paper* theme — placed in a 1990s context.

The social conservative position, in effect, is that the oppression and poverty pinpointed by socialists are best resolved through dependence on the market rather than on a "command economy." It often communicates the image that it is short on compassion. Moreover, social conservatism is sometimes more narrowly defined as opposition to a range of ideas, such as abortion and gay rights. Fiscal conservatism, in that context, relates only to economics and not to social issues. Manning maintains that, as defined in *Political Realignment*, social conservatism takes into account both fiscal and social matters.

On 18 March 1967, the *Edmonton Journal* carried the text of the *White Paper* synthesis along with a photo not of the premier but of his son, with the caption "Among the Report's Architects." One paragraph, headed "New and Old," noted:

These new concepts and the new policies based on them are the outcome of exhaustive analysis of knowledge and experience gained from the past. To the best of our knowledge, the fundamental principles on which these new concepts and policies are based are verities which will remain constant, notwithstanding the ever-changing circumstances and conditions which call for new and different applications of old and enduring truths.

As time passed, Preston and his father set up M and M Systems Research Ltd., later changed to the simpler Manning Consultants Ltd. Most of their work with the energy industry involved the "softer" issues despite Preston's interest in the financial side of the business. Community relations, environmental impacts, and the interface with Native groups were important.

Under these various structures, Preston honed his mind and skills in the areas of conflict management, communications, community development, and political realignment. He worked at conflict management through contracts that involved bringing together oil companies and Native groups.

It was in that setting that the remarkable story of Ernestine Gibot emerged. Her story was fully told in the October 1984 issue of *Reader's Digest* by Bob Collins, the former editor of *Imperial Oil Review*. Preston refers to Ernestine's sojourn in *The New Canada*. And in doing so, he reveals his deeply held belief that extraordinary individual efforts to resolve conflict are often the best antidotes to the failure of the state to keep its social safety net mended.

As far as Manning Consultants was concerned, Ernestine's story began

> when Geneva Ensign, who was involved in evaluating a government-sponsored Native Women Employment Training Program, came to my office. She brought with her a Chipewyan woman named Ernestine Gibot, who eventually taught me at least half of what I know about Indian people and the social welfare system.

A residential school that separated Ernestine painfully from her parents for years, an eighteen-year marriage that included living in shacks and tents, nineteen pregnancies and fourteen live births, poverty, drinking, abuse, sickness, and hopelessness were all in her background when Manning met her in 1974.

After she found her first self-sustaining job, in 1980,

Manning retraced with her the steps she had taken and the network of agencies with which she had dealt. That network included hospitals and treatment centres, government agencies, the city jail, churches, Native training programs, and a vocational college. Manning writes:

> I noted that this complex network of "helping systems" delivered certain services effectively — health care, financial support, accommodation and training. At the same time, it failed to provide guidance at critical times or to offer encouragement, incentive and employment. The people who really helped Ernestine during this period were often individuals she would not have met had she not been "in the system." However, in order to truly help Ernestine, these individuals often had to step outside their professional roles and act on their own initiative, rendering services above and beyond those called for in their job descriptions and sometimes in violation of the system's rules.
>
> This was the case, for example, with the doctor and the priest who said: "We shouldn't really be saying this, but you should leave the north and leave your husband if you want to live."
>
> . . . I also found it significant that Ernestine's first impression of the potential helpfulness of a government agency or program was not based on its literature or the credentials of its personnel but simply on the attitude and friendliness of the secretary or receptionist guarding the door or answering the phone.
>
> While I learned a great deal from Ernestine that was helpful to me in assessing the impact of the Esso heavy oil plant on the Indian bands of northeastern Alberta, I also learned that Ernestine desperately wanted a job — a real job. It became a personal and corporate challenge for me.

Manning told Ernestine that, when some white people get fired or can't find a job, they do not go around saying they are unemployed. Instead, they get cards printed that say they are a "consultant." Ernestine was sceptical that such an idea would work for her, but she decided to give it a try. Her card identified her business as Ernestine's Counselling Services. Manning had two reasons for suggesting that designation. First, his survey of her volunteer activities showed that she had spent considerable time visiting Native people in hospital who needed comfort and counsel. She could speak to them in five languages — English, French, Cree, Chipewyan, and Slavey. Second, she had counselled Preston deeply in the understanding of Native ways — and the lessons that suffering teaches.

In *The New Canada*, Manning continues:

> On 12 September 1980, I came into my office to find a message on my desk from (my executive assistant) Jeanie Clemenger, written in big red letters. The message was "Ernestine has a Job!" She had been offered a position as a native liaison worker with the school board and was soon promoted to teacher's aide. It had taken seven years from the day Ernestine had decided to start a new life until the day she got a full-time job that paid a working wage.

Manning later wrote the experience into a presentation for Manning Consultants' Economic Development Discussion Group, entitled "A Job for Ernestine." It became a focal point for finding ways for individuals — white or Native — immersed in their systems to shorten the job paths for the Ernestines of the future. "At the end of the session," Manning notes, "Ernestine dropped by to say a few words. We never applaud presentations at the EDDG, but that morning there was a departure from the rule." The subsequent story of Ernestine was a combination of heartaches (sickness and violent deaths in the family) and triumphs (including the *Reader's Digest* story that inspired other Native women to follow in Ernestine's footsteps.)

Preston Manning's community development "laboratory" was Slave Lake, a northern Alberta town that became an opportunity for him to test his ideas on what a community could become through a close working relationship between government and the private sector. In *The New Canada*, Preston says his work on the *White Paper on Human Resources Development* triggered the Mannings' interest in Slave Lake. The paper identified the south shore of Lesser Slave Lake, 150 miles north of Edmonton, as one of the most underdeveloped parts of the province. Ernest Manning's Socred successor, Harry Strom, initiated some community development projects there, and it was a special area under federal regional-development legislation. Moreover, it was potentially part of the oil patch.

A group of six Slave Lakers approached Ernest Manning not too long after he was out of power, asking him and Preston to join a "community development company" for the region. The six were Slave Lake mayor and grocer Leo Boisvert, town councillor and bush-air-service owner Mel Zachary, provincial human resources development coordinator Neil Gilliat, Sawridge Native Band chief Walter Twinn (now a senator), Alberta Research Council industrial engineer Jim Ergil, and Pacific Western Securities vice-president Stan Kendall. The group believed that Slave Lake, as gateway to north-central Alberta, had enormous economic and human potential. They wanted to use the proposed company to get people to participate directly as investors and project initiators in social and economic development.

The Mannings liked the idea because the group was not waiting for a government rescue effort, as was so often the case with underdeveloped communities. And they liked the prospect of linking economic and social objectives. Recalls Preston Manning:

> Almost everything I know about the people and special challenges of resource-industry service towns — and there are literally thousands of these in Canada — I owe to the people of Slave Lake, my fellow directors on the board of Slave Lake Developments and our community development adventures in north central Alberta.

For twenty years, Preston was in Slave Lake at least once a month for SLD meetings and other project activities. He discovered that Slave Lakers did not particularly relish people coming in with what they claimed to be altruistic motives. They more easily trusted those who acted in enlightened self-interest. Manning Consultants made sure, for example, that it charged a consulting fee, although it withheld collection on it until SLD was in a position to pay. Today Preston might call that approach compassionate common sense.

Understanding people meant dealing in everyday reality rather than with simple theory. One of the people who became Slave Lake mayor was a young woman named Val Merideth. Later she moved to the West Coast and became active in Reform in Surrey-White Rock. In 1993, she was elected MP for the riding. Merideth can be tough when she wants. She sustained a broken marriage not long before being elected to Parliament, and she maintains that her Christian faith and support base helped her to keep her head together under considerable pressure.

With that in mind, I was interested to listen to an unrehearsed talk she gave in a seminar following the 1996 National Prayer Breakfast, whose theme was "understanding." Those sessions are off the record in the interests of preserving the privacy of MPs as they grapple across party lines with the spiritual issues that affect their political activities.

The speaker of the day was David Lam, the Christian Hong Kong-born former lieutenant-governor of British Columbia. During his tenure, Lam's straight-talking with B.C. residents of both Caucasian and Asian descent was seen as a major factor in the relatively smooth handling of the pre-1997 Hong Kong influx into Vancouver. At the prayer breakfast, Lam talked about understanding and reconciliation, emphasizing the need to understand where those who are different are coming from.

The evening before, a leadership session had been addressed by Wally McKay, a First Nations leader on the aboriginal task force of the Evangelical Fellowship of Canada. McKay had told of the wrenching effects on him of leaving his parents for the first time to attend a residential school. When he became a born-again Christian, he found it hard to give up the drums and the traditional Native prayers. Today, in maturity, he had said, he intended to make a drum and share with his church, in a Christian context, some of those traditional prayers and songs.

In responding to what she had heard, Merideth spoke of her Slave Lake days as a time when the whole framework for understanding was being developed, almost subconsciously. And for her, the gospel, as reflected in the Manning approach, helped in the process of change brought about by community development.

Preston Manning recalls with amusement the dialogue between him and Imperial Oil president Bill Twaits, when he asked the company for a $25,000 "social investment":

I hurriedly explained the concept — that we had a group of people in Slave Lake who wanted to develop their community through private enterprise, that they had raised some capital through local share sales, that they needed some joint-venture partners to capitalize a project to house oilfield workers, and that they hoped to buy out their joint-venture partners in a short while if the project was a success.

Twaits wanted to know why SLD didn't go to Imperial's charity people. Manning's reply: "Because these people don't want charity or a government grant. They want investment capital on which their project will pay a return." So why not go to the oil company's real estate people?

> Because I know what kind of return your real estate people will be looking for, and this project can't deliver it. We want you to take a portion of your return in the form of a social benefit — better housing for your field people in Slave Lake and some community good will. That's why we call it a "social investment."

Eventually, Twaits came through with the money, but he insisted that, as far as he was concerned, it was charity, not an investment. Similar money was obtained from several other oil patch firms.

In due course, SLD was able to pay back the money as promised. A Calgary luncheon was the scene of the hand-over of cheques. After the lunch, an executive from one of the companies receiving a cheque approached Preston, saying, as closely as Manning could recall: "Look, none of us expected to get this back and we've already written it off. Could you find some charitable project up there we could donate this money to?" The SLD directors huddled and then told the oil patchers that the Slave Lake seniors wanted to build a drop-in centre and would happily receive a contribution. And so that "social investment" went back to Slave Lake.

For me, peering into the Manning mind-set with respect to Slave Lake shone some light on their approach to what is often called "social justice" in left-leaning Christian circles. Social justice Christians often urge governments to intervene in economic matters to see that a social safety net is in place. One left-leaning evangelical, who did not want to be identified because he values his friendship with Preston, told me that he was disappointed that the Reform leader seemed unable to exhibit compassion. Another decried the lack of "social action" shown by either Ernest or Preston Manning. But Manning prudence would dictate that "if it ain't broke, don't fix it." And, more to the point, if it is broken, then it needs fixing, not social engineering. So what seems like a nonsolution to a left-leaner may be seen more accurately as a solution that works without a lot of fanfare and revolution.

Many reporters see a similar "nonaction" in Manning's seeming lacklustre performance as leader of the unofficial opposition. But others point to the fact that Reform's very presence has caused the Liberals to carry forward a shadowy resemblance to a Reform-like agenda of deficit reduction and free market policies. The Liberal approach, says Preston, is to "ignore, then ridicule, then attack, and finally adopt" Reform proposals.

In the fall of 1996, he started to press for a tax cut when deficit reduction reaches a certain point. His approach draws ridicule, but it keeps in front of Canadians the concept that many social problems solve themselves if people have more individual control over their own earning and spending activities. And much of this thinking goes back to Slave Lake. In *The New Canada*, Manning suggests:

Some day, an economic historian will do a thorough case study of the economic and social development of north central Alberta, paying attention to the relative

contributions of the federal and provincial governments, the private sector (particularly the oil and
forestry companies) and the local players (especially
the municipal governments, the Indian bands and the
local entrepreneurs and businesses). The anecdotes
and lessons on grassroots economic development contained in the minute books and files of Slave Lake
Developments would be a valuable contribution to
such a study. At the corporate level, there would be the
story of knocking on the doors of 35 mortgage companies before obtaining the first commercial mortgage
money for an office building in Slave Lake. At the
community level, there would be the story of the fire
in townhouse no. 37 (total value of the fire/smoke
damage, $500; damage caused by the antics of the
volunteer fire department, $5,000). There would also
be the story of SLD's one serious business failure, an
unsuccessful attempt to rescue the local GM dealership
during the crash after the National Energy Program,
and all the personal heartache these types of failures
entail in small towns.

Preston Manning ghostwrote large sections of his father's
best-selling book *Political Realignment: A Challenge to
Thoughtful Canadians* (1967), which enunciated the social
conservative concept. The book sold thirty thousand copies,
by any measure a runaway success in a nation where five
thousand copies sold was pretty good. Part of the success,
of course, related to the bulk order by Alberta and Ontario
Conservatives for distribution before the federal Conservative leadership convention in 1967. Headlines in Alberta
newspapers often simply began "The Book." While it was
only one hundred pages in length, its authorship seemed,
for a few weeks at least, to lend to it some of the lesser
attributes of holy writ.

The premier's last cabinet

...like any other except for cameras

Ernest Manning, Tuesday presided over his last regular cabinet meeting as leader of the Social Credit Party.

Premier Manning's day was just like any other but there were cameras on hand, and especially warm smiles and greetings from his staff when he arrived for work Tuesday morning about nine o'clock.

Next week the Social Credit Party will name a new leader from five candidates seeking the top job.

Voting will take place Friday evening, Dec. 6.

The premier has announced there will be a cabinet meeting Dec. 10. He will still be premier, serving out his final hours, but insisting she will be party leader.

Mr. Manning has been premier of Alberta since 1943 and is the second Social Credit swept to power under W. Blair Aberhart in 1935. Mr. Manning succeeded Mr. Aberhart.

Chance to say goodbye

Members of the Socia. Credit caucus will get their chance to say goodbye to Premier Manning Tuesday, Dec. 3.

The premier is expected to let caucus members about his immediate plans.

He will likely tell them he will step down from his new post, making way for a 'nobleman in Strathcona East. Then he is expected to take a lengthy holiday before returning to Edmonton and going to work full-time, promoting his theories of political realignment.

At the premier's last cabinet meeting as leader was Lands and Forests Minister A. J. Hooke, who came to power with the premier in 1935.

It is still expected Mr. Hooke will enter the leadership race.

Candidates for leadership are Municipal Affairs Minister Harry Strom, Education and Labor Minister Ray Reierson, Highways Minister Gordon Taylor, Attorney-General Edgar Gerhart and the MLA for Clover Bar, Dr. Walter Buck.

PREMIER ARRIVES AT LEGISLATURE

'CAN THESE FIGURES BE CORRECT?'

Journal photos
by Stan Fruet

READY FOR DAY'S WORK

NOW THEN, GENTLEMEN . . .

9. *Edmonton Journal* spread on Ernest Manning's
last cabinet meeting, on 26 November 1968.

Political Realignment, following the Manning penchant for conveniently numbered, easy-to-follow outlines, suggested there were four stages in the Canadian experience through which the two major political parties passed in a sort of evolutionary process:

1) Decades ago, there were major differences between the Liberals and Conservatives, and people could vote according to their personal convictions.

2) When one party became dominant, however, the other, wanting to gain power, watered down its principles. That led to "convergence." Personality, more than identifying principles, became the vehicle that gave the parties their movement.

3) Then came the disintegration of the traditional party system. To Ernest Manning, the inadequacy was that no party could meet the obvious requirements of the country. That gave rise to third parties, such as the NDP, consisting of people who wanted a political movement that stood for something at least.

4) The fourth stage involved reformation. (Remember, this book was written two decades before the rise of Reform.) Out of the chaos, Manning hoped, the fragmented structure would re-form, polarizing into two parties. One would be clearly conservative, while the other would reflect what he called the "welfare state philosophy."

The Mannings hoped that the realignment would allow the social conservative party to dominate, for two reasons. First, it would attract the Conservatives, most Socreds, and many right-leaning Liberals — as well as some who, for whatever reason, were outside the political process. Second, the left side of the spectrum was potentially helpful in identifying social issues that needed resolving. But it would take a party strongly committed to the private sector and personal initiative to successfully address the concerns raised by the left.

The Mannings never expected everyone to go social conservative. The reality, they understood, was that there would always be a left side on the spectrum, fuelled by the class struggle and a sincere belief in the merits of state control.

The book concluded the assessment of the federal political scene with the following paragraph, entitled "Consideration of One Remaining Alternative":

Anyone who speaks or writes on the subject of political realignment is open to the common misinterpretation that he is advocating the formation of another political party altogether apart from those presently in existence. I wish to make it very clear that this is not what I am advocating in this thesis. I do not believe that the formation of an entirely new political party is the best way to meet the serious national political needs of the present hour. Nevertheless, having regard to the prevailing mood of the Canadian people, present national party leaders and federal politicians, especially those affiliated with the Progressive Conservative Party of Canada, should take cognizance of the following fact: if the Canadian political situation continues to degenerate, and if the cause of conservatism continues to suffer and decline, not for lack of merit or a willingness on the part of the Canadian people to support modern conservative principles or policies, but rather because of unnecessary dissension among politicians and parties, the idea of establishing a wholly new political party committed to the social conservative position will find an ever increasing number of advocates and supporters among a concerned and aroused Canadian public.

Preston Manning maintains today that much of what he was able to do in the 1960s would never have flown under his own flag. His father was the door opener. But more than that, he was the sounding board, the rewrite man, and the encourager to his son. In the best sense, they used each other.

The evidence, in retrospect, was the treatment given the book at the time by two respected establishment journalists, Peter C. Newman and Bruce Hutchison. Both suggested that the federal Conservative Party — then on the eve of choosing a successor to John Diefenbaker — needed to take notice of the "social conservative" proposal, the book's central thesis. Hutchison, writing on 23 August 1967 in the *Free Press Weekly*, suggested that the Alberta premier had "planted his private time bomb in politics and it will explode in due season — not because he has invented a new idea but because the existing situation cannot continue long."

A quarter of a century later, both journalists would write dismissively of both Preston Manning and Reform. In the months before his death at ninety-three, Hutchison wrote several columns for the *Vancouver Sun* expressing his profound dislike for all that Reform and its leader seemed to him to represent. Newman, for his part, wrote derisively in 1995 in *The Canadian Revolution* of Manning's "Howdy Doody chin" flapping away in the leadership debates leading up to the 1993 federal election. His comment was only pages away from his chiding the Conservatives for exploiting Jean Chrétien's facial paralysis in television commercials run during the same election campaign. (In fairness to Newman, it should be noted that he wrote neutrally in the 24 February 1997 issue of *Maclean's* about department store magnate Fred Eaton's support for Manning. Maybe the central Canada establishment tide was beginning to turn.)

That the Mannings tackled a federal political-realign-
ment question, rather than a provincial one, should not be
surprising. Many Canadian political observers saw the
Manning government as a model for effective political
action that could be contextualized federally. In short, they
wanted Ernest Manning to become prime minister. Some
saw his becoming a Conservative and succeeding Diefenbaker as the way to go; others thought that he would be a
suitable replacement for Robert Thompson, national Social
Credit leader.

But Ernest Manning kept his own counsel. He was not
above listening to the national siren call. He knew there
were people of influence throughout the country who
respected his Christian presence and believed that his
faith had a lot to do with his reputation for integrity and
competence.

In *The New Canada*, Preston Manning writes that his
father's response to the idea of entering federal politics was
"that he was not [interested] but that he did have some
views on how federal politics might be realigned." Those
views became "The Book." Preston continues:

> The central thesis of the book was that Canadians
> deserved some real choices in federal politics, and that
> these were not offered by the current alignment of
> parties. My father then outlined a philosophical posi-
> tion, described as "social conservatism," which was a
> synthesis of marketplace economics and some of the
> social concerns of humanitarian socialism. He used
> the term "synthesis" rather than "compromise" to
> distinguish the position of social conservatives from
> that of the "Red Tories," who were just then beginning
> to emerge within the Progressive Conservative ranks.
> He challenged the federal Conservatives to realign
> themselves along this axis, asserting that if they did so,

the realigned Progressive Conservative Party could prove to be an attractive home for supporters of the federal Social Credit Party and federal Liberals who were uneasy about the leftward drift of their party. His candid analysis of the limited future of the federal Social Credit Party hastened its demise, which was already impending, and paved the way for the federal Social Credit leader Robert Thompson to align himself with the Conservatives.

Preston's mention of Thompson is worth exploring in the interests of what ultimately flowed from The Book. Thompson, originally a teacher in Alberta, became a Socred during the Aberhart years. After war service in the air force, he became an evangelical Christian missionary in Ethiopia and was, in due course, seconded to Emperor Haile Selassie's government to help rebuild the country's educational system. Returning to Canada, he entered federal politics and became the national Social Credit leader. His most significant time on the federal scene came when the Socreds and NDP shared the balance of power in what he later described as the "House of Minorities." That scenario occurred from 1962 to 1968, during the successive minority governments of Tory John Diefenbaker and Liberal Lester Pearson.

The religious theme is worth exploring for a moment. The four party leaders in the House of Commons at the time were all — to varying degrees — evangelical Christians who made their faith part of their way of doing politics. Thompson, a member of the Evangelical Free Church, was probably the closest theologically to the Mannings. Tommy Douglas, who had by then "graduated" from the Saskatchewan premiership to become the first federal NDP leader, remained an ordained minister of the Baptist Union of Western Canada. Diefenbaker was a faithful member of

First Baptist Church of Prince Albert, affiliated with the same group. And Pearson was a serious Christian in the United Church tradition; his father had been a United Church minister with Methodist roots. In a sense, the four of them were forced to draw on the conciliatory aspects of their common faith in order to prevent an unnecessary election, particularly during Pearson's tenure.

Thompson, now eighty-three, recalls that Diefenbaker was the most prickly to deal with. A rather independent sort, he seemed to see sinister motives in any attempt by a political rival to make common cause. By contrast, Douglas and Pearson were more inclined to play ball. "In fact," Thompson recalls, "there were times when Pearson and I prayed together." The minority situation resulted, he believes, in some very good social legislation.

That religious mix was an exception to the rule. Mackenzie King was a Presbyterian who dabbled occasionally in spiritualism and seances. After him, except for Diefenbaker, Pearson, and Kim Campbell, the prime ministers have been Roman Catholic: Louis St. Laurent, Pierre Trudeau, Joe Clark, John Turner, Brian Mulroney, and Jean Chrétien. All have been passingly to moderately devout and well schooled in the values of their faith. Chrétien self-effacingly enjoys reminding people who doubt his piety that he has to live up to his name, which, translated into English, is "Christian."

Preston Manning's fleeting reference to Thompson deserves further amplification. In the early 1970s, Thompson, noting the ageing process in the national Social Credit and the inability of its western and Quebec wings to get along, figuratively folded Social Credit into the federal Conservatives. The Trudeau Liberals had been in power for just a few years. Thompson, who was then MP for Red Deer, had moved to the West Coast for the sake of the health of several of his adult children, who had Down's syndrome. In the 1972 election, he ran under the Tory banner for the first

10. Grandpa Ernest (left) and his brother, Bill (right), with Ernest's grandchildren in October 1983 at the Rosetown farm, where Ernest committed his life to Christ after hearing a radio sermon by "Bible Bill" Aberhart.

11. Ernest and Preston Manning, both wearing
their Reform Party lapel pins, in 1988.

time, in Surrey-White Rock, losing narrowly to popular *Vancouver Sun* columnist Barry Mather, an NDPer.

More significantly, the new Conservative leader, Robert Stanfield, had appointed Thompson national campaign director for the Tories. In that capacity, he crisscrossed the land — to the possible detriment of the campaign in his own riding. In the end, he snatched defeat from the jaws of victory; the Liberals beat the Conservatives 109 seats to 108.

But the groundswell had begun. Much of the increased Tory strength was from the west. And much of the swing in votes came because evangelical Christians were prepared to follow Thompson into the Tories.

Alex Paterson, a minister of the Nazarene church, was one example. In the 1960s, as Fraser Valley East MP, he was a Thompson Socred. In the 1968 election, known as the Trudeau sweep, Liberal poultry processor Gerry Pringle replaced him, mainly because the Tories and Socreds split the vote. But in 1972, coming back as a Thompson Tory, Paterson regained the seat and held it for another thirteen years. He was followed by Ross Belsher, a department store executive and treasurer of the Sevenoaks Alliance megachurch in Abbotsford; he held the seat for two more terms.

Meanwhile, Benno Friesen, an English teacher at Trinity Western, the Christian university in the Fraser Valley that Thompson had helped to found, was tutored by Thompson to run in Surrey-White Rock. He did run, and he held the seat until he retired in 1993. Both Surrey-White Rock and Fraser Valley East were taken that year by evangelical Christians who were Reformers: Val Merideth and Chuck Strahl.

Friesen does not particularly like the rise of Preston Manning, even though he shares his faith. Friesen reflects some of the hurt felt by Conservatives who had been encouraged into politics by Thompson that Manning did not do the same. His sense was that Manning parlayed unfair and cynical criticism of Brian Mulroney into a platform for his own political success.

Ross Belsher took a different approach. He saw the Conservative decline as inevitable and only somewhat related to the rise of Reform. And he was happy enough with Chuck Strahl that he passed on both his constituency office and some of his staff to his successor.

It is time to get back to Preston Manning's father. After his retirement from the Alberta premiership, Ernest Manning accepted several corporate directorships and an appointment to the Senate, where he sat for thirteen years until mandatory retirement at age seventy-five.

Both the Senate appointment and a CIBC directorate represented, for many of the older Socreds with whom Manning had built the party, something of a betrayal. William Aberhart, after all, had railed against the big banks and the concentration of political and corporate power in central Canada. His and Manning's early political success had come in part from their ability to tilt at the powerful central windmills. And Manning's accepting the Senate appointment was unsettling to some because it had been offered by Pierre Trudeau, the man whom many westerners considered a socialist — perhaps even a closet Marxist.

Manning's Senate experience provided for his son a good deal of information about the federal scene that would come in handy later. Particularly useful were his obser-vations on the Upper House and its role in the Canadian political system. They provided a backdrop for Reform's support of what is known as the "Triple-E" Senate. Under Triple-E, the Senate would be "elected, effective, and equal." Stripped of its alliteration, the idea is that the Upper House should provide equal representation for Can-ada's five regions. It would thus enact a balance against a Lower House configured to favour the heavily populated central regions over the hinterlands.

All these developments, then, paved the way for Preston Manning to begin building the Reform Party. After a side trip to explore some of the religious-political influences in other parties, we will trace the Reform story.

CHAPTER 9

Parallels in
Faith Leverage

POLITICAL PUNDITS often assume that the religious influence Ernest Manning brought to Alberta politics was an aberration. Perhaps because the influences were from the then-despised evangelical minority, rather than from mainstream Protestantism or Catholicism, they stood out more.

My objective in this chapter is to put the case that there were — and are — parallels in mainstream religion of faith leverage on the political system. Some of that religious mentoring comes not so much from direct father-son relationships as through church educational or fellowship systems.

While writing this book, I happened to watch the live coverage on CBC Newsworld of the funeral of Joe Ghiz, premier of Prince Edward Island during the last half of the 1980s. The son of Lebanese immigrants, Ghiz was a brilliant orator whose place on the national stage came during the Charlottetown Accord talks, when he eloquently defended both Canadian unity and what he perceived to be Quebec's special place within Canada. The similarities and contrasts between the funerals of Joe Ghiz and Ernest Manning were both striking and significant. Each drew about 1,200 people. Ghiz's state ecumenical funeral took place in the gothic splendour of St. Dunstan's Basilica in Charlottetown and was attended by Prime Minister Chrétien. The officiating clergymen were gowned. The liturgies of Canada's mainstream churches — Catholic and Anglican — were studiously followed. Ghiz's wife, mother, daughter, and son sat quietly in the front row. References to the relationship between Ghiz's faith and political life were implicit rather than explicit. The eulogy included a reference to times at the family cottage when — a good cigar in hand and a couple of Scotches and a barbecued steak under his belt — Joe would regale the gathered clan with warmly told political tales. And there was some speculation that Ghiz's university-student son might follow in his father's political footsteps.

By contrast, Ernest Manning's funeral was in sleek, windowless, fifteen-year-old First Alliance Church in Calgary. The ministers wore business suits. The only federal politicians in sight were Reform MPs. The service exuded evangelical informality and included eulogies from Manning's son and one of his granddaughters, Andrea Manning, who noted: "For us kids, Grandpa was our source of history, knowledge, and encouragement.... You could expand your knowledge and understanding of life, love, relationships, achievement, business, law, and politics just by watching him and talking to him." His serious commitment to balancing faith and political action was made clear. The service was videotaped and later run on *100 Huntley Street*, the Christian talk show hosted by Pentecostal communicator David Mainse. Preston Manning's eulogy ran in full in the *Globe and Mail*.

But the similarities between the funerals were intriguing. Both services were strongly Christian, biblical, and emotionally moving.

Particularly striking at Ghiz's service was the choice of scripture, especially a passage from John's gospel noting, in Jesus's words, "I am the way, the truth and the life; no one comes to the Father, except by me." That passage affirms in the strongest terms the evangelical verity that was part of Ernest Manning's faith — the uniqueness of Jesus among the world's religious leaders. Christian theologians have argued for centuries that the ability of Christians to live by Christian values rests in their personal commitment to God the son. And that, in essence, was Manning's message each week on the *National Bible Hour* each year for fifty years. The two funerals help to define, in some sense at least, the east-west solitudes with which Ernest Manning dealt — and in which Preston Manning finds himself.

Prince Edward Island is old Canadian establishment, where Europeans settled and brought their culture long before Confederation. Alberta did not become a province until 1905. Most of the European settlement did not begin until the turn of the century. Furthermore, the discovery of oil began a new, technologically driven era of development.

Christianity has been — and continues to be — an influence in Canada, but its expression is often shaped by the predominant culture of each region. The cultural factors result in a range of emphases, with Christianity taking on different hues in different places.

Ernest Manning emphasized the individual side of faith. It was thus consistent for him to stress less government and more individual responsibility. His emphasis was on the life-changing effect of commitment to Jesus Christ. And he wanted his listeners to understand that their parents, church, or good works could not make them into Christians. As individuals, they were responsible for their own spiritual condition and destiny.

In the longer-established mainline churches, predominant in eastern Canada, there is more emphasis on the importance of the Christian community in shaping the individual. Parents are reminded that, when children are brought for baptism, church and family enter into a contract to spiritually nurture those offspring.

In both paradigms, however, there is another side to the picture. In the evangelical churches that played such an important part in Ernest Manning's life, there is, behind the emphasis on individual responsibility, a strong sense of community. Conversely, in the established churches, where community is emphasized, there is a muted but nevertheless distinct acceptance of the importance of the individual.

The Ghiz and Manning funerals provide some interesting comparisons that hint at those faith-leverage parallels to which I referred earlier. A few more examples follow.

Many Canadian politicians have received a Jesuit education, particularly in Quebec. Even in the west, there have occasionally been similar examples.

One was Dave Barrett, the British Columbia NDP premier from 1972 to 1975 and later a Member of Parliament. Barrett grew up in a Jewish home, and his mother was a strong Marxist. His university education was in Jesuit schools in the United States, a fact to which he continuously testified. A major mentor in the Jesuit system was Thomas Aquinas. And Barrett — though he has remained an agnostic — often paid homage to the Aquinian influences that were part of his education.

There is another interesting case — the 1986 story of former Liberal leader and short-term prime minister John Turner. The story is recounted by Roy McGregor, then of the *Toronto Star*, in *Asking Questions — the Art of the Media Interview*, a textbook edited by then Ryerson journalism teacher and former CBC news producer Paul McLaughlin. Looking for an interesting angle on Turner at the time he was running for the Liberal leadership, McGregor had heard that his favourite summer reading subject was theology.

He learned, in fact, that Turner would read several versions of the Bible to develop his insights. He queried the future prime minister on the subject during the 1984 Liberal leadership race. Notes McGregor:

> I found I had a whole package that had to do with religion. [Turner] believed in sacrifice. [He believed] that God gave you certain rewards on earth with the idea that you some day return them even if it costs you. And that's why [in 1986] he's still in there fighting [as opposition leader]. It's the religion that drives him, not the ambition.

I want to add one more recent report, this one with respect to Quebec. In November 1996, a book by Diane Francis, editor of the *Financial Post*, was released by Key Porter Books. Entitled *Fighting for Canada*, it makes the case that the Parti Québécois and the separatist movement are descendants of a long-time anti-English, anticapitalist Catholic secret order known as La Patenté. She suggests that the Jesuits — or at least their philosophy — have shaped two hundred of the separatist elite in Quebec and, by so doing, exerted a good deal of influence on the province and the nation.

On 30 November 1996, Don Macpherson, provincial-affairs correspondent for the Montreal *Gazette*, debunked her allegations as paranoia. Francis indicates, however, that the potential influence of La Patenté and the Jesuits is worth putting on paper at least. And from this perspective, the book's value is to propose that in Quebec, as in Alberta, the religious influences on politics have been — and remain — strong. The difference lies in the fact that the influences come from different branches of Christianity — one old and established, the other new and, in the view of some, schismatic.

I will wrap up this chapter with four more examples, from the current House of Commons, of people whose faith surfaces occasionally. All four are Liberals. They are open about their faith perspectives — and they let them emerge naturally, without pretence. The four are industry minister John Manley, junior Pacific Rim minister Raymond Chan, speaker Gib Parent, and deputy speaker David Kilgour.

Manley, an Anglican, has written movingly about his "making Cursillo" and the impact it had on his faith. Cursillo is a movement within Anglican and Roman Catholic churches that nurtures people into faith in much the same way that Bible study groups do in evangelical churches. In *Double Vision: The Inside Story of the Liberals in Power*, Edward Greenspon writes about the way in which Manley's faith works in his political life, in his seeing to it that people are listened to and treated properly.

Raymond Chan worships at a Chinese Mennonite Brethren church in the Vancouver suburb of Richmond, British Columbia. In his prepolitical days, his faith shaped his activism in China affairs, particularly at the time when Tiananmen Square was in the news. That activism likely played a role in drawing Jean Chrétien's attention to Chan's interests and skills.

Gib Parent is a Roman Catholic and does not mind being known as part of the community on Parliament Hill that periodically prays together. Politicians on all sides of the house attest to his fairness and moderation in the speaker's chair. He has publically spoken of his asking God for guidance, especially at times when the house is a bit unruly.

David Kilgour's main opportunity to share his faith with the nation came in October 1994 during an evangelical prayer rally video-linked to several cities across Canada. Kilgour emphasized the importance of Bible study in his life and expressed appreciation for the gift of a study Bible that was of considerable help to him at the time in his spiritual pursuits.

Kilgour, who happens to be John Turner's brother-in-law, was a Conservative MP for some years before switching to the Liberals. He contrasts a bit with Preston Manning in the way he does politics. Both men represent Alberta ridings. Kilgour has chosen to settle his family in Ottawa, where he centres his social life and attends church (McKay United, an evangelically leaning congregation across the street from Rideau Hall, the governor general's residence). He visits his riding as necessary to handle his constituents' needs. Manning, conversely, maintains his family in Calgary and tries to get home every weekend. The Mannings attend church there and tend to steer clear of the Ottawa social scene.

That might be one reason why Manning, after several years in Ottawa, still seems like an outsider, while Kilgour is often seen as being someone out of touch with Alberta. Whatever the relationship of facts to that perception, the Christian faith of both men shapes the way they do their political tasks.

CHAPTER 10

Embarking on an Adventure

IN HIS ARCHIVAL INTERVIEWS, conducted around 1980, twelve years after leaving the premiership, Ernest Manning suggested that Preston was waiting for the right party to come along before entering the political fray.

As a physics student at the University of Alberta, Preston became increasingly restive. Most of his studies related to physics and math, and he recalls that he had little contact with the university's political science, economics, and history departments.

While Preston had, out of a sense of duty to the Socreds, once sat as a backbencher in the university's model parliament, he was not among the political movers and shakers on campus. But he readily identifies those who were: Joe Clark, who led the U of A Conservative club; Jim Coutts, leader of the campus Liberals, who went on to become principal secretary to Pierre Trudeau; Grant Notley, who headed the school's New Democrats; and Ray Speaker, the campus Socred leader. Notley, who later became NDP leader in Alberta, was killed in a plane crash in 1984.

Speaker went on to become a cabinet minister in both Harry Strom's Socred regime and Don Getty's Conservative government and then a Reform MP in 1993.

In describing his transition, Preston notes:

> By the end of my third year, I had become convinced that I should change faculties. My academic interests were broadening and I found it harder and harder to focus exclusively and successfully on math and physics. This was a rather stressful time for me. I had invested so much time and energy in the physics program, I was loath to give it up. I was also by no means certain as to what future direction I should take.

He says his religious training sent him to the scriptures to seek God's direction. That he did, as well as broaden his reading beyond the sciences for the first time in three years. He remembers reading the *Journals* of John Wesley, the founder of the Methodists, and being envious that Wesley had absolute certainty about his mission in life. Only much later did Preston learn that Wesley was over thirty when he discovered that mission. Preston himself was only twenty-one.

He occasionally admits to checking the calendar, recognizing that his political timeline and his father's have been quite different. At the age he started Reform, his father had been in provincial politics close to a quarter century and was approaching the status of one of Canada's longest-running premiers.

Switching to economics, Preston also spent a pivotal summer in San Francisco working for Bechtel Corporation rather than on the family farm, as he had the two previous summers. At Bechtel, he had a close look at the pure science side of the operation as well as its business-government relationships.

So it was that, when he finished his B.A. in 1964, Preston set his sights on consulting work rather than undertaking graduate studies. But on the way, he spent three years working informally on a range of projects in which his father was interested. One project was a cross-country speaking tour in connection with Ernest Manning's sense that Canada needed a "national spiritual awakening" like those that had gripped the eastern seaboard of the United States and various European countries decades before. Preston notes:

> I studied the Protestant Reformation, the first and second Evangelical Awakenings in Great Britain and the American revival movements, as well as the theology of "spiritual awakenings" as described in the Christian scriptures. Then, my friend, Ed Kennedy [son of Orvis Kennedy, long-time right-hander to the elder Manning in both Socred and *National Bible Hour* matters], went on an extended cross-Canada speaking tour to churches and youth groups that had an interest in the subject.

Preston took a stab at federal politics in 1965, running in Edmonton East for the Socreds and ending up a distant second to Conservative Bill Skoreyko, who had first been elected seven years before in the Diefenbaker sweep. During that period, the Conservative and Socred competition was splitting the centre-right vote in western Canada, a point that was not lost on the Mannings when, later in the decade, they collaborated on *Political Realignment*.

One point of enlightenment that Preston picked up in that 1965 run was the ethnic diversity of Edmonton East. He did not see Canada as necessarily a nation composed of two founding races. That might have been the view from Ottawa, Montreal, and Toronto, but it was from the Edmonton East perspective that it began to dawn on him that Canada's linguistic and cultural heritage came from three equally divided sectors: English, French, and neither. (And it was during his Slave Lake experience that he caught on that there were half a million aboriginal people in Canada and that they were here first.) So, all along, the groundwork was being laid for Preston Manning's political activity, specifically the start of Reform.

Preston goes into some detail about the development of the Reform Party in *The New Canada*.

In brief, its seeds were nurtured in the years following the 1984 election of the Mulroney Conservative government. The Tories' decision to award the maintenance of Canada's fleet of 136 CF-18 fighter planes to Canadair of Montreal, even though Winnipeg's Bristol Aerospace bid came in $3.5 million lower, at $100.5 million, was critical. The Tory victim was the key Manitoba cabinet minister, Jake Epp, who, coincidentally, was viewed by many evangelical Christians as their pipeline to Mulroney. Epp was left with the task of explaining to westerners that the CF-18 decision was in the national interest. That explanation was parodied by Les MacPherson in a sports column in the Saskatoon *Star-Phoenix*. He suggested that, even though the Calgary Flames had won the Stanley Cup, it should go to the Montreal Canadiens. MacPherson had Brian Mulroney conceding that Calgary had the best hockey team, "but we have to support Canada's hockey industry, which is centred in Montreal, [and is] in the best position to take full advantage of the Stanley Cup."

By 1986, a number of disparate western voices were expressing the need for a western Reform movement, including the Canada West Foundation and *Alberta Report* publisher Ted Byfield. In September 1986, Preston Manning wrote a memo to Byfield entitled "A Western Reform Movement: The Responsible Alternative to Western Separatism." His self-confessed intention was to "get some discussion going." The upshot was an invitation to speak at an Alberta "doers" group in November on a proposal to create a western-based political party to run candidates in the 1988 federal election.

Soon afterward, Manning met with Stan Roberts, the former president of the Canada West Foundation who was by then president of the Canadian Chamber of Commerce. Out of that discussion came a decision to set up what became the Western Assembly on Canada's Economic and Political Future the following May in Vancouver. The Vancouver Assembly, as it became popularly known, drew over six hundred. Before they parted ways, they approved setting up a steering committee to plan a founding assembly for a new party, six months later in Winnipeg. Both Manning and Roberts were on that committee.

Awaiting his scheduled plane following the assembly, Manning watched a hockey game with Ken Whyte, then with *Alberta Report* and now editor of *Saturday Night*. The game was auspicious for embryonic Reformers. That night the Edmonton Oilers won their third Stanley Cup.

If Reform's conception occurred in Vancouver, its birthplace was in Winnipeg. There its name was chosen, its constitution and principles were hammered out, and its first leader was elected. It was not quite a cakewalk for Preston. Roberts contested the election but withdrew at the last minute. He died two years later of a brain tumour. Manning recalls him with respect, as a long-time servant to both the west and Canada.

By the 1988 election, the Reform Party was able to run candidates throughout western Canada. Preston ran against his old friend, Joe Clark, in Yellowhead and came a strong second. But it took a later by-election and a precedent-setting Alberta senate election to form the first Reform "caucus" in Ottawa. Deborah Grey took the by-election in Beaver River, and the late Stan Waters won the senate vote, later reluctantly confirmed by Prime Minister Mulroney.

12. Ernest Manning, Deborah Grey, and Preston Manning, applauding former Manitoba Premier Douglas Campbell (out of camera range), then in his nineties, at a March 1989 dinner in Calgary honouring the Beaver River by-election win that put Grey in the House of Commons.

I watched most of these proceedings from a distance. But I had two meetings with Preston in the mid-1980s, and they gave me some insights into what was happening in his mind at least.

One was at his and Sandra's big rancher overlooking the Sturgeon River valley in St. Albert, just north of Edmonton. He, Sandra, and all five of the children were at the noisy — yet orderly — table eating hamburgers. After supper, we retreated to the family room and watched a ball game. Gradually, the conversation, at that point between Sandra, Preston, and me, turned to the prospect of developing a new political movement.

At the time, I was based in Vancouver, editing a monthly tabloid that was distributed to several hundred Vancouver-area churches. Preston was on the board of Regent College, an evangelical graduate school of theology at the University of British Columbia. He taught the occasional workshop on decision-making, demonstrating the concepts with some computerized "what if" decision tree models. And he and Sandra took some summer school courses at Regent. Doing so was part of their continuing quest to figure out how to do politics Christianly and to be reconcilers in an adversarial society.

At St. Albert, Preston spoke of two small-group models that had proved effective in the launching of movements. One was William Aberhart's approach — that of bringing together people in the 1930s, in hundreds of groups across Alberta, to study the concepts of Social Credit. The other was the trend, in evangelical churches, to divide the church into small groups. These groups fostered bonding on a more personal basis — the building of community — in the interests of learning about the church. The groups brought together people who were new to the faith with more seasoned members. The regular meeting of the groups meant there was continuity in the learning process. In due course, the sense of community brought about the growth of a church-centred movement that would give impetus to outreach. Some of that outreach would involve finding unmet social needs in the community and developing projects to meet them.

The small-group process intrigued Preston. At that time, he thought it could be one of the keys to the successful development of a new political movement. Sandra took a wait-and-see approach. And Preston valued her approach because she was more naturally outgoing than he. He would study the model, and she would have a gut feeling on its workability.

Be that as it may, Preston considered setting up small groups of interested people throughout British Columbia and Alberta. And, he noted, some of his interest in the group idea had come from courses he had taken at Regent College. He wanted to see if the concepts that spurred on spiritual growth in churches could be utilized in the 1980s to rouse dormant political awareness.

My other meeting with Preston took place in late 1986. I had taken a short-lived position as an editor at *Alberta Report*, the successful conservative/Christian magazine run by Ted Byfield and his family. During a lunch meeting in a hotel restaurant a few blocks from the AR office, Preston pulled a sheaf of sixteen pages out of his briefcase. The cover sheet, marked "draft" in the top right-hand corner, was titled "Proposal for the Creation of a Western-Based Political Party to Run Candidates in the 1988 Federal Election." The document listed several western concerns, such as economic injustice, a reference to what was commonly described as the "$100-billion heist," known in central Canada as the National Energy Policy. The draft left the clear implication that many of the west's difficulties had begun with Pierre Trudeau and were not being corrected, as had been hoped, by the Mulroney Conservatives.

13. Christmas in Arizona, 1986. From rear left,
Grandpa and Grandma, Nathan and David, Sandra and Preston.
Front, Mary Joy and Avryll. Andrea took the picture.

Ironically, it was Trudeau who had appointed Preston's father to the Senate in the early 1970s. Ernest Manning would only agree to the appointment if he could sit as an independent, as neither a Liberal nor a Conservative. There were clear indications, from time to time, that he was a valuable conduit of information to some of the western groups looking for political reform. As a senator, he had only a modest profile. But his views were not ignored for a moment by many of the westerners who wanted change — including his son.

The draft document also traced the "reform tradition in western Canada," from the Riel Rebellion, through the Progressive Party, to the Depression parties of Social Credit and the Co-operative Commonwealth Federation (CCF), and it ended with a question: "The next Reform movement?" While the document stressed the need for a western party, Manning suggested verbally that there was a commonality of hinterlands in Canada. And they might rise up in due course and challenge the national strangleholds of the business, media, and political elites in the Toronto-Ottawa-Montreal triangle. Tensions between hinterland and power base were not limited to the west. Even the Quebec separatist movement was stronger in the hinterland than it was in downtown Montreal, where non-French ethnic groups and "the English" tended to want to stay in Canada.

I returned to the AR office and told Ted Byfield about the lunch meeting. Within days, he arranged a dinner meeting with Manning and several AR journalists. It was not long before AR stated its support for Reform, on the basis of its conservative leanings and Manning's personal stand for Christian values. But throughout the years, the magazine has not refrained from criticism of Reform, particularly if the party has shown more interest in populism and moderation than in conservatism.

14. Campaign respite: Preston's nonpolitical football.
It was a common sight on airport tarmacs during the
1993 election to see Preston tossing a football
with campaign aides and even airplane pilots.
(Photo by Dave Burton)

As Reform took shape under Preston Manning's leadership, some of the policies and practices that emerged seemed to be 1990s versions of Ernest Manning's way of doing things. Their similar approach to social issues, especially those on which hot discussion never ceased, is a case in point. Ernest practised total abstinence from alcohol, and so does Preston. Yet the elder Manning governed a province that wanted to liberalize drinking laws in an era when prohibition was a painful memory. Out of that crucible came a very workable formula for standing up for the issues one believes in while ensuring that democracy prevails.

Whether it involved a vote in the house or a referendum put to the people, Ernest Manning operated on the following four-part premise when making decisions on social or moral issues:

1) Give the house — or the people — the chance to speak and vote on the issue.
2) Engage in a dialogue with the people, during which you exercise your right to persuade them of your views.
3) Find out what the community consensus is through the vote or an accurate polling process.
4) If there is a consensus, vote according to what the people want; if not, vote in line with your own conscience. The key here was the word "consensus." Strong views more or less evenly split did not represent a consensus and shifted responsibility back to the member to vote according to his or her conscience.

Ernest Manning had strong views about the damage liquor could do in a society. He believed the biblical proverb that declares "wine is a mocker and strong drink, a brawler, and whoever is intoxicated by it is not wise." He was prepared to use moral suasion — and a few well-chosen statistics — but would not try to impose his standards on the population. In fact, as a populist, he saw it as serving God adequately only when he served the people well.

In *The Dynasty: The Rise and Fall of Social Credit in Alberta*, John Barr comments on the biblical rationale by which Ernest Manning reconciled his own views with the will of the people:

> No one really dared openly accuse Manning of promoting his religious views for political purposes; Manning was too obviously sincere. [He] demonstrated on several occasions that he would not allow his personal religious views to influence important policy questions — the matter of liquor, for example. Alberta's liquor laws, once primitive (although no more so than in many other provinces not run by fundamentalists), were rapidly updated after the late 1950s [to be] probably about on a par with most in Canada.
>
> Manning referred to this problem obliquely in a *National Bible Hour* broadcast on February 5, 1966, which was devoted to the theme that "in any unregenerate society, the will of the people is bound to come into conflict with the will of God."
>
> Referring to the Israelites in I Samuel, who, in spite of God's will expressed through the prophets, wanted a king, Manning noted that God instructed Samuel to "protest solemnly unto them and show them the manner of the King that shall reign over them," which Samuel did.
>
> The people, however, were unmoved and Samuel reported this to God, who replied: "Harken unto their voice and make them a King." The lesson drawn from this by Manning was that when the will of the people conflicts with the will of God . . . the people must be allowed to have their way, for only by having their way

and suffering the consequences will they come to see the error of their prideful stubbornness.

This emphasis in Manning's life was criticized by some, but generally speaking, it contributed to his image as an honest, sincere, upright man, a leader who could be trusted almost absolutely.

By the time Preston Manning was politically active, the hot social issue was no longer liquor but abortion. And the Sue Rodriguez case indicated that euthanasia and assisted suicide were not far behind. On a personal basis, Preston is pro-life, so he opposes both abortion and assisted suicide. That he maintains it as a *personal* view is often unsatisfactory to militant anti-abortionists and pro-abortionists alike. But as the populist son of a populist father, he sees the will of God for him as seeking the will of the people.

Essentially, Preston has provided his father's formula to Reform MPs for decision-making on moral or social issues. In that context, he has raised the ire of pro-lifers on occasion because he has admitted the possibility that he might vote in the House of Commons in favour of abortion — even though he is personally opposed to it. But the key to his modest enthusiasm for the formula is that it encourages communication between the member and his or her constituents. Discourse and dialogue, with their potential for increasing understanding and exploring the depths of the values held, are natural parts of the process. One does not need to be a staunch evangelist to share one's values with the community. A member of Parliament is privileged to do so and should not shun that honour, Manning believes.

Preston Manning often made the point, before he had a seat in the House of Commons, that he wanted to bring a conciliatory approach to an adversarial system. But he knew that such a lofty objective was a long shot. Conflict

15. Preston and Sandra Manning's first walkabout
on Parliament Hill, shortly after the 1993 election.

resolution has been in vogue for some years in the corporate world, but the parliamentary system seems to thrive on keeping the conflict going as long as possible.

In Reform's early years, Preston liked to refer to a hockey analogy. He said Reform had a right wing, left wing, and centre. The right wing was represented by fiscal conservatives in the party, while the left was represented by members with strong social concerns. The centre, in effect, helped to reconcile the two wings. "And we are all shooting for the same goal," he used to point out. But some of his followers were uncomfortable with the analogy. They used to warn their leader: "You can let those left-wingers skate up and down the ice if you want. But please don't ever give them the puck."

When Reform ended up with fifty-two seats to the Bloc Québécois's fifty-four after the 1993 election, Manning waggishly suggested that the Bloc would be Her Majesty's somewhat less than loyal opposition, while his party might be known as "Her Majesty's Constructive Alternative." It was his way of establishing, at the beginning, that he would try to do what he could to fit the conciliatory peg into the adversarial hole.

Within that context, we will take a look at Manning's leadership philosophy and style as they have worked themselves out in the present Parliament. Three events are worth exploring: (1) Manning's call, after the Quebec referendum, for impeachment proceedings against Prime Minister Jean Chrétien; (2) Manning's handling of the Bill C-33 debate and his subsequent actions to curb some outspoken members of the Reform caucus; and (3) Manning's speeches to the press gallery and to a Washington, DC, audience.

Shortly after the 30 October 1995 referendum in Quebec, Manning called for the possible impeachment of Chrétien, thus evoking a strong emotional response. His point was that Chrétien had come within a hairbreadth of failing to defend Canada against the onslaught of the separatists. In the view of his critics, Manning was using an American word, one that had only been used in the memory of most of them with respect to Richard Nixon. Furthermore, Manning was accused of stepping out of character. Here was the reconciler using inflammatory language. Was he not a hypocrite?

The fur flew for a few days. Then a strange thing happened. Some media pundits suggested that, although Manning was indeed talking out of character, his point was worth considering. Craig Oliver, CTV's Ottawa correspondent, was particularly eloquent in noting that Manning was not speaking out of ignorance but had an excellent grasp of political history. Manning admitted that he had overstated the case. Yet several major media made the point that in a democracy the prime minister is accountable to the people.

Perhaps the toughest time for Manning came in the spring of 1996, when Bill C-33 was debated in the House of Commons. The bill, piloted by Justice Minister Alan Rock, banned discrimination in certain government agencies on the basis of sexual orientation. That provision was added to several others, including discrimination based on religion.

The word around Parliament Hill was that homosexual leaders had been lobbying heavily for passage of the bill. Many MPs in all the parties had been feeling the pressure. Several Liberals had spoken out against the bill. Reform had done so as well, but it had emphasized only that any human rights bill needed to ensure equality for all citizens.

In the process, two Reform MPs were "smoked out" by reporters and made comments about gays that, on the surface, were clearly discriminatory. Interestingly, for those who had hoped that Bill C-33 would pit Christians against gays, the two MPs in question did not share Manning's evangelical Christian convictions. Manning suspended the two from caucus and let the issue cool down for a few weeks, until the party's assembly in Vancouver later in the spring. In some of his public statements, he came as close as anyone had seen to losing his cool. Some wondered if the death of his father had deprived him of a good sounding board on such matters.

At the assembly, Manning made the strong point that Reformers had to guard their tongues if they were to be fit to assume power. He did not blame the media, although he could have singled out some journalists for using ambush tactics unevenly — in other words, more on Reformers than on Liberals. And he kept hammering away at the equality issue. The weakness in Bill C-33, he insisted, was that groups not named in the legislation could more easily be targeted for discrimination than those that were named. In pointing that out, he knew full well that religious affiliation now had the same protection under the law as did sexual orientation.

Some insight into Manning's handling of Bill C-33 and its fallout can be gained by taking a look at talks Manning gave on 14 March and 2 May 1995, respectively, to the Heritage Foundation in Washington, DC, and to a Canadian Press panel in Ottawa on "Gotcha Journalism."

In Washington, Manning talked about the similarities and differences between reform movements in Canada and the United States. (Because he met with Newt Gingrich, Reform later got a reputation for being a Canadian version of hard-right American politics.) Manning noted that in Canada political reform became visible in 1987 with the formation of the Reform Party. South of the border, it started with the "Perot phenomenon prior to the 1992 presidential election and is now embodied in the new Republican majorities in Congress and the Contract with America."

The similarities between Canadian and American reform, Manning said, are found in a "profound loss of faith, on the part of large numbers of people, in the capacity of big governments to provide economic and social security for citizens. The primary emphasis, in both nations, has been on reducing or limiting government overspending, debts, deficits, and overtaxation."

Among the differences were that reform in the United States was being led by a traditional party — the GOP — that was reforming itself, whereas in Canada the traditional Conservative Party had nearly been wiped out, and the reform impetus was coming from a third party. Moreover, fiscal conservatives in the United States are usually also conservative on moral and social issues, while in Canada that connection is not so well defined. Manning continued:

> It seems to me that Reformers in Canada need to be careful that in rejecting the state-enforced values of the welfare state (anti-family, pro-abortion, soft on crime, liberal on homosexual rights and euthanasia) we don't simply propose to replace those values with another set of state-enforced values, more to our liking but still imposed from the top down.
>
> Now the remedy that Canadian Reformers propose to this dilemma is to prescribe a heavy dose of *democratization* to public decision-making on moral issues, and trust we can persuade the majority of our fellow citizens in a fair, democratic decision-making process to do the "right" thing most of the time. (On moral issues, at least two doses of democracy to one of ideology.)

In his comments to the Canadian Press panel, Manning stressed the need to deemphasize the left/right/centre approach to economic issues, the socialist/liberal/conservative axis in federal politics, and the partnership-of-racial-groups approach to national identity and unity.

16. Parents and grandparents fête Avryll (in white, foreground),
graduating in nursing from the Southern Alberta Institute
of Technology. In rear is older sister, Andrea, a lawyer.

17. Grandma and Grandpa with Nathan, on the occasion
of his high school graduation in June 1995. Nathan is
the same age as Ernest Manning was when he left
Rosetown to attend Calgary Prophetic Bible Institute.

I have noted that Reform's "friendly critic," Tom Flanagan, a political scientist at the University of Calgary and
former Reform policy director, is critical of Manning's
having apparently gathered so many evangelicals around
himself. His argument is that the party should be more
clearly conservative and less populist in nature. However,
in a January 1994 article in *Politics: Canada*, a political
science journal, Flanagan is a little less critical. He notes:

> Manning is undoubtedly a business-oriented free mar-
> keteer, but not in the same thorough-going, consistent
> sense as, say, the Fraser Institute or the National
> Citizens' Coalition. As a political leader, Manning's
> business is winning votes and attracting support, not
> maintaining ideological purity.
>
> Murray Dobbin, a hostile critic of the Reform Party,
> has emphasized Manning's penchant for "calculated
> ambiguity." But the ability to be ambiguous is a talent
> that all political leaders must develop, and one need
> not be a hostile critic to note that Manning possesses
> it. A close look at Reform's positions shows that many
> of them contain important qualification, balancing
> factors or escape clauses. For example: a Reform
> government will balance the budget in three years or
> "it will call an election."
>
> [B]ecause no new party has a chance to win seats if
> it merely echoes what existing parties have on offer,
> Manning has assumed some provocative positions in
> order to break into the political system.
>
> But in personal terms, he is anything but an extrem-
> ist, dogmatist or ideologist. Of 20th century political
> leaders, William Lyon Mackenzie King offers the best
> comparison. Manning has a much greater sense of
> humour than the earnest, self-righteous Mackenzie
> King, but he has a similar sense of mission, intellectual

bent, introverted personality, patience and ability to obfuscate issues in the course of achieving political objectives.

That, then, is Tom Flanagan's view.

My own observation, based on a number of conversations with both Preston and Sandra Manning, is that the American system provides him with another role model, one who fits better than either Newt Gingrich or Mackenzie King. His name is Jimmy Carter.

In the late 1970s, Carter served one term as president of the United States. Although somewhat less conservative politically than Manning, he is a devout Southern Baptist, and was able to beat Gerald Ford in part by attracting the "born again" vote, which often goes to the Republican Party. Preston's view of the role of Christian reconciliation in the political process lines up more with Carter's than with virtually any other known North American political figure.

Much of Carter's postpresidential work has been in the field of conciliation. Some of it, like his work in Haiti and the former Yugoslavia, has been widely reported. Indeed, many of his friends waggishly suggest that Carter is the only person ever to have used the American presidency as a stepping stone to a better job.

Preston Manning knows that he must do his best to bring to power, or at least to official opposition status, the party that he founded. But if that is not in the cards, then it is safe to say that there will be a conciliatory role for him to play. And I would not underestimate his ability, whether in political office or not, to do something worthwhile for Quebec-Canada relations.

If that should be the scenario, he would have on his hands a challenge that proved to be too much for other westerners, notably Joe Clark and Robert Thompson. Preston has often made the point, however, that westerners should be good reconcilers because they, as much as Quebeckers, understand what it means to be alienated from the national psyche.

In the closing chapter, we will try to pull all these strands together to see if they offer any prophetic glimpses into Preston Manning's future.

CHAPTER II

A Prophetic Glance Ahead

BY ATTEMPTING TO DEFINE social conservatism and developing a party that reflects that blend, Preston Manning has picked up where his father left off. Two 1996 news items will help us to focus on the challenges that the younger Manning faces in carrying his modification of his father's vision forward.

One was a good-humoured Canadian Press story of 28 May 1996, headlined in the *Vancouver Sun* as "Preston's Youngest Son, David, Reforms Dad's Idea of What Makes Good Music." The story, by Jennifer Dutchburn, told about David Manning's involvement in a rock band called the Buicks, whose influences include reggae, the soft-punk music of the Clash, and pop supergroup U2. Both he and his older brother Nathan and some cousins play in the band in a variety of settings, including churches.

Not much has been written about Preston and Sandra Manning's five children, now ranging from late twenties to midteens. The daughters are the oldest and are well into their own careers and, in the case of Andrea and Avryll, their

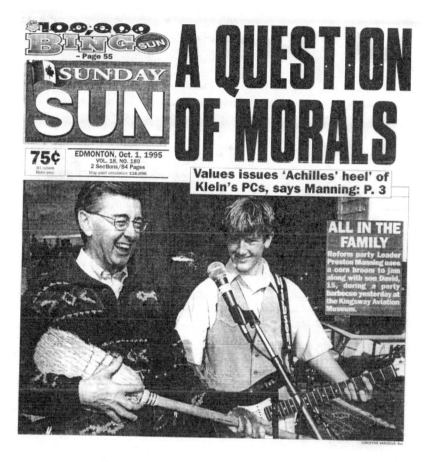

18. *Edmonton Sun* front page of 1 October 1995 captured Preston with a corn broom "jamming" with his guitar-playing younger son David during a Reform Party barbecue.

19. *Calgary Herald* front page of 20 February 1996, the day after Ernest Manning's death at eighty-seven.

marriages. But each of the five has been encouraged and assisted by Preston and Sandra to take up some short term Christian service in another part of the world.

The eldest, Andrea, a lawyer, spent time with Action International working with street kids in Manila. Avryll, the second, nursed in a Zaire camp for Rwandan refugees with Christian Children's Fund. Mary Joy worked for several months in the Niger office of SIM International, a long-established evangelical mission agency. Nate helped to build a school in Bethlehem after attending a Teen Missions boot camp in Florida. David's turn will likely come this summer, with a Teen Missions stint in Asia. And some wags who know the family think that David's rock band is as much a cross-cultural experience as anything the other children have done.

All the Manning children share their parents' faith and respect their political involvement. And Preston cherishes the times when he and Sandra can share their values with them.

Perhaps some of the Manning children or in-laws will find their way into politics. Their education and family experiences have paved the way for that possibility. But the greater likelihood is that they will spread themselves out into many corners of community influence. For Preston, he was the only son who could develop and carry out a political vision; his brother, Keith, had a special role circumscribed by his physical restrictions. But Preston and Sandra produced five children and provided them with the combined resources of his sense of innovation and her gregarious nature. That combination stretches their possibilities.

But who might succeed Preston Manning politically? This question brings into play the second story referred to earlier, that of Stephen Harper's decision to leave the Reform Party caucus. It would not be fair to draw a tight comparison between the William Aberhart-Ernest

Manning link and that involving Preston Manning and Stephen Harper. After all, Preston had sons — Bible Bill never did.

There is no question, however, that Harper, now thirty-seven, moved from agnosticism to a serious Christian commitment between the time he first considered political involvement and the mid-1990s. In a December 1995 article in the *Ottawa Times*, a conservative, Christian-influenced paper, Jonathan Bloedow quotes the former Calgary-area Reform MP as suggesting:

> "Twenty years ago, when I was a teenager, I would have been an agnostic, central Canadian liberal. And my life experiences have led me to come to other conclusions about both life and political values — both intellectually and spiritually."
>
> Religiously, he says, "I am a Christian. I wouldn't say I have a well-developed theology, but my personal religious views, which I tend not to make much an issue of publicly, would probably be categorized as conservative Christian views.
>
> "I was raised in the United Church, but my parents are fairly conservative in a religious sense and have left the United Church. I am an adherent [to] the Alliance Church, but I am not a member at the moment."

In evangelical parlance, Stephen Harper has been "nurtured" or "discipled" by an evangelical Christian in the Reform Party — perhaps by more than one, because there are seventeen other evangelicals, about one-third of the caucus, who are likely capable of nudging him along in his pilgrimage.

Until recently, Harper was seen as a possible successor to Manning (along with Deborah Grey, also an evangelical Christian). But that prospect is thrown into question because Harper has resigned from the Commons and is now working with the National Citizens' Coalition. Perhaps he doesn't see a leadership vacancy in the next few years and is saving his political energy for later. After all, that is what Jean Chrétien did in leaving the Liberal cabinet during the Trudeau years. Harper claims that he is not running again because of family. His reason is worth taking at face value because his newly adopted faith would compel him to stay close to and care for his young family. But he will likely take some time to keep Reformers aware of him so that, when the time is ripe, he will be there.

Meanwhile, Preston Manning, who has personified Reform and shaped it so completely during its first few years, will work toward bringing the party into official opposition — perhaps even government. He will certainly continue the quest begun in those early-1970s brainstormers with Don Posterski and Don Page. Doing things "Christianly" will mean working consistently at reconciliation and conflict resolution. If anything about the differences between his situation and his father's bothers him, it is that, like his father, he prefers solving problems to being adversarial — and in opposition that is tough.

But opportunities for conciliation are there. One came in April 1995 at the National Prayer Breakfast, an annual Parliament Hill tradition. Manning was asked to lead the morning's prayer. Knowing that party leaders are usually entrusted only with scripture readings, not prayers, at the breakfast, he took the responsibility seriously. He linked his own understanding of faith with that of the multipartisan group in thanking God for "answered prayer." Manning cited the recovery of his archrival Lucien Bouchard, then the Bloc Québécois leader, from a bout of the life-threatening flesh-eating disease. That recovery, he suggested, was a widely understood example of God's penchant for answering prayer. Afterward, he pointed out that answered prayer is, for many people, what brings them to faith. The conciliatory aspect to his action is that, despite political differences, many people of faith in all parties prayed for Bouchard during his crisis. Manning had the insight to make that link.

In the same year, Manning admitted to the *Canadian Baptist* that he often feels God has placed him in an "utterly secular place" where the mind-set of the major decision-makers is relatively devoid of a "spiritual dimension." And that is why little events, such as the linking of Bouchard's recovery to the sense that there is a prayer-answering God, are so important to the nation's spiritual development.

The same God, Manning believes, can speak to a politician's personal need, whether engendered by illness, self-doubt, or a broken marriage. And to him, that kind of God lifts the cloud of oppression, bringing reconciliation when it is least expected, most needed, or both.

In considering Manning's future, we need to take into account the *National Bible Hour*. A shift in responsibility for the radio program that introduced the teenaged Ernest Manning to Calvary — and Calgary — occurred in 1990 when a Buffalo-based mission with a Canadian branch office in St. Catharines took over the assets and the vision of the NBH and blended them into its own structure.

Six years later, in the summer of 1996, the Honourable Ernest C. Manning Building was dedicated in St. Catharines to the glory of God and the continuing work of Global Outreach Mission, the organization that had taken over the broadcast. The building is a modest enough two-storey, neocolonial, red-brick structure. It houses the Canadian headquarters of GOM and NBH. And money from the space rented out to several small businesses is put back into the ministry so that the drain on the evangelical donor dollar is minimized.

Few of those whom Preston Manning refers to as the Canadian political elites have likely ever heard of Global

Outreach Mission. But its role in extending Manning's view of Christian ministry into the twenty-first century is worth noting.

Jim Blackwood is a Canadian who first came in contact with the Mannings close to forty years ago when he was the front man for Barry Moore. An Ontario-based school-teacher who became an evangelist, Moore was once a household name in many small-city evangelical homes by virtue of the crowds he attracted to hockey rinks across the country. Eventually, Moore went international and became much less known in his own country.

In due course, Blackwood became involved with Global Outreach Mission, which intriguingly enough in light of Preston Manning's arm's length relationship with Quebec, does much of its radio work in that province, as well as in France and the French-speaking countries of west Africa and the Caribbean. The Quebec broadcast activity involves twelve stations; that beamed into francophone nations works through an additional thirty. Furthermore, GOM carries out Bengali radio broadcasts in Bangladesh. And in addition to its radio activity, it has a traditional missionary force of 329 people working in thirty-two countries. My use of the term "traditional" reflects GOM's commitment to the idea that it is quite in order to cross cultural barriers to communicate the Christian gospel. Technologically, however, the means of communication are cutting-edge. In addition to using radio in a 1990s way, the mission specializes in aviation and medical projects that link social concerns to the gospel in many of the world's less "developed" nations.

The addition of the *National Bible Hour* arrow to GOM's quiver reflects a recognition of current reality. Ernest Manning's ministry slowly declined as Manning grew older. (It is estimated to have once had a Canadian audience of 500,000, larger than the number of people in this country who listened to comedian Jack Benny.) And furthermore,

20. The Honourable Ernest C. Manning Building in
St. Catharines, Ontario, Canadian headquarters for Global
Outreach Mission, which took over *Canada's National
Bible Hour* from the Mannings in 1990. Preston spoke
at the dedication of the building in the summer of 1996.
(Global Outreach Mission photo)

the advent of television brought about a more dramatic and often expensive way of communicating the gospel. In Canada, David Mainse of *100 Huntley Street* in Burlington, John Hull of The Peoples Church in Toronto, Willard Thiessen of *It's a New Day* in Winnipeg, as well as Terry Winter and Bernice Gerard in Vancouver, all became skilled at attracting moderately large audiences. Moreover, there was a proliferation of Canadian and American evangelical radio programs where once Manning shared the ether with no more than half a dozen. Well into the 1980s, though, he continued to have a loyal — if ageing — audience of at least a few thousand a week.

But with the daunting task of developing Reform, Preston was not about to take over the radio ministry too. As he often noted later, people in the 1940s were willing to tolerate a political leader preaching the gospel on Sundays. But their progeny would not. "Can you imagine what the *Toronto Star* would do if Mike Harris conducted a mini-crusade for Christ today?" he asked rhetorically at the dedication of the building in St. Catharines named for his father.

But Jim Blackwood knew that the *National Bible Hour* had a new niche to fill. Those Quebec and overseas high-tech ministries needed people and money to run them: people prepared to leave all and follow Jesus to the ends of the Earth, and money from those who stay behind and tithe their incomes to support those who go abroad. So in bringing NBH into the GOM fold, Blackwood was marrying the traditions of yesteryear with a vision for gospel communication in the twenty-first century.

When Preston Manning spoke at the dedication of the St. Catharines building, he knew his task was to bless that marriage. Blackwood warmed up the crowd of two hundred people, most with greying or balding heads. He told how Ernest Manning took over the broadcast when William

Aberhart "went to be with the Lord." He spoke of thousands who "found Jesus Christ as personal Saviour" and of "homes reunited." He described Manning as one of the great "expositors of scripture in the Dominion of Canada." All these phrases resonated with an older evangelical audience because they reflected spiritual reality for them.

When Preston went to the podium, he declared that he intended to engage in both a little nostalgia and some vision-casting. He started with a self-deprecating joke about Baptists. It seems, he said, that some small-town Baptists, like their contemporaries worldwide, held strong and divergent opinions. In their Bible class one Sunday, they had a heated discussion about the right thing to do if marauders were to attack the family home. The group agreed that the wife and children should be hidden in the basement and that the husband should face the roving band. But they disagreed as to whether the man should tell the attackers the truth or a lie about where the rest of the family was hidden. The outcome of the discussion was the formation of a new Baptist church in the town. Henceforth, the two churches were to be known as the "truthful Baptists" and the "lying Baptists." As a second-generation evangelical, Manning enjoys twitting his fellow believers about their idiosyncrasies, which would be subject to rude ridicule in the outside cynical world.

Then, warming to his theme, Preston spoke of his father's conversion and the role that radio had played in getting him into politics. He gave a little lecture on the clear distinction — perhaps clearer on the Prairies than in other parts of Canada — between churches that stress the social gospel and those that emphasize "personal salvation." When you entered the home of the social gospeller and pick up the family Bible, he said, it will fall open to the parable of the Good Samaritan, who loved his neighbour as himself. And when you go to the home where personal salvation is emphasized, the Bible will fall open to John 3.16: "For God so loved the world, that he gave his only begotten son, that whosoever believes in him shall not perish but have everlasting life."

Manning then spoke of the maturing process in Canadian Christianity that had led many "social gospel" churches to investigate the emphasis on a personal relationship with God. And, conversely, many evangelicals had become serious about how their faith impacts on their relations with others.

Preston also spoke of his father's analytical mind and his ability to come up with three-point, five-point, or seven-point sermons. But always, he noted, no matter what biblical passage Ernest Manning "exposited," he had the following seven points to make:

1) Human beings are separated from God.
2) That separation results from ingrained evil.
3) God the Son was the mediator, taking on himself both sides of the dispute.
4) Christ opened the way to reconciliation.
5) That reconciliation came through the crowning act of sacrifice at Calvary.
6) Jesus was raised from the dead as a sign that God the Father accepted his sacrifice on humanity's behalf.
7) Personal faith in the person, words, death, and resurrection of Christ brings acceptance of the human being before God.

As he emphasized the final point, Preston betrayed the fact that, though this set of beliefs was at the heart of his own being, he had to lay aside his logical, systems-based thinking to embrace it. He noted: "We don't understand the mechanics by which we become accepted by God. But we know that what starts out as an act of faith becomes that by which things actually begin to happen."

Committing one's trust to a person, rather than simply to a creed, is not a foreign concept, Preston suggested. His illustration was the story about his father's relationship with J. Howard Pew, the patriarch of Sun Oil. In the late 1950s, when the development of the Athabaska tar sands was first contemplated, Pew visited Alberta to see what he could do.

At issue was whether the two men could trust each other. Pew's ideas about extracting the oil from the sands were just a few of the many put forward — and some were "pretty weird." Could Manning trust Pew? Could Pew trust Manning? At the time, Alberta could not sell all its traditionally produced oil. It was a buyers' market.

But Manning and Pew learned that they had something in common: a trust in Jesus Christ as personal Saviour. And, incredibly, that trust was enough for Pew, then over eighty, and Manning, then in his fifties, to shake hands on the banks of the Athabaska River. It sealed a deal that would begin the task of extracting the oil, whose reserves are calculated to be considerably greater than those of Saudi Arabia but considerably more expensive to exploit.

So much for the nostalgia, Preston told his St. Catharines audience, as he launched into his vision-casting. And for that he went to the George Rawlyk–*Maclean's* survey of 1993, in which two-thirds of the 4,500 Canadians polled said they believe in the divinity of Jesus. The survey also indicated that fifteen percent of Canadians claim to be born-again Christians. That Manning included Rawlyk's work as part of his look to the future, in speaking to this relatively conservative evangelical audience, attested to his penchant for Christian conciliation. Rawlyk, head of Queen's University's history department for years, was an evangelical who chronicled the history of the movement with consistent dedication. And he was a lifelong social democrat who, in his early years, wrote press releases for Tommy Douglas. Furthermore, the last book he wrote before his death in a car accident was entitled *Is Jesus Your Personal Saviour?* It was an account of the interaction between his research and his spiritual pilgrimage.

Manning's message to GOM, which still runs tapes of his father's sermons at least once a month on sixty stations in the Canadian market, was one of hope. Blackwood admits that the NBH audience continues to age, but Manning's point was that there are still many Canadians of all ages who are open to consideration of the Christian faith.

As Blackwood recalls the conversations in the 1980s with Ernest Manning, with respect to a GOM takeover of the broadcast, he appreciated the former premier's pleasure that the mission did much of its work in Quebec in French. "He told me that, in retrospect, the *National Bible Hour* should perhaps have developed a French broadcast for Quebec years ago." Furthermore, Blackwood suggests, Manning had an interest in missions and Christian development work that never really came through in the broadcast. So he was happy that the NBH's new stewards were involved that way.

As missions go, GOM is neither large nor small. Its annual budget is three million dollars. Its support base in Canada comes mainly from Fellowship Baptist, Associated Gospel, and Plymouth Brethren churches. The charismatic wing of evangelicalism is not part of the mission. And GOM operates a little closer to the fundamentalist sector than most evangelical Christians, including Preston and Sandra Manning and their five children.

But Blackwood was delighted at the content of Preston's talk:

> Many of our people were not even sure that he was a committed Christian. And he was masterful in the way he linked the past with the future. I just wish we could get the video of his address out to the evangelical

churches of Ontario before the next [federal] election. We are not political, but it would help people to understand that Reform has a leader who is able to bring a Christian perspective to the affairs of the nation.

On 23 February 1997, Preston addressed a different kind of audience on faith issues. In a dinner sponsored by fellow Alliance church member Kevin Jenkins, former president of Canadian Airlines International, Manning talked to one hundred Alberta leaders in Calgary about doing leadership Christianly on moral issues in a pluralistic society. He made the point that this talk reflected forty years of thinking.

Manning used the story of the devil's temptation of Jesus to point out what Christian leaders should *not* do. Jesus, he said, rejected overtures that on the surface would give him image, power, and the resources to do what he wanted.

In talking about what Christian leaders *can* do, he encouraged the concept of "speaking the truth in love" with as much emphasis on the latter as on the former. Deeply held values get better acceptance if they are communicated with authentic love, rather than being "rammed down the throats" of others. Manning saw that point as important because, so often, in an adversarial political process, hostility is seen as the only effective means of communication, but its results are counter-productive.

And the Christian leader, having said and done what he or she believes to be right, will leave the results up to God, Manning concluded. He suggested that such an attitude provides a sense of peace and effectively reduces the frustrations leaders experience when they try to control the whole process themselves.

Manning has made it clear, as we saw in the last chapter, that he wants to lead a party that is willing to govern Canada. But he keeps reminding himself and others that

21. Some of the people who have helped the Reform Party to grow:
a) National Citizens' Coalition vice-president Stephen Harper,
who might one day be the leader; b) Past executive council
member Gordon Wusyk, who introduced former Canadian Airlines
president Kevin Jenkins to evangelical faith. Ultimately, Jenkins and
Preston Manning joined First Alliance Church in Calgary and have
become good counsellors to each other on matters religious and political; c) Lawyer, candidate recruiter, organizer, and long-time
Manning family friend Virgil Anderson; d) Originally from
Nigeria, Ed Onyebuchi of Winnipeg joined the party because
he liked Preston's generally unrecognized understanding of
international matters. Preston comes by that understanding
because of his strong interest in Christian-based international
missions, relief, and development; e) Skier Nancy Green Raine,
who doesn't mind admitting to her party membership.

someone committed to reconciliation might need to accept sacrifice in a larger cause.

Preston and his father talked about the kind of reform that would coalesce around social conservative ideas. Robert Thompson introduced the process that more or less replicated that situation within the Conservative Party, which parlayed the replication into nine years of government. But there is no such coalescing now on the federal level. Some fiscal conservatives — such as David Frum — have suggested that the Reform Party and the Conservatives will someday merge. And, more recently, Tom Flanagan and Stephen Harper have suggested what amounts to a strategic alliance between the Reformers and Tories. Could that happen with the present leadership of the two parties?

It was tried before. When Thompson headed the national Socreds, they had a Quebec element known as the Creditistés and headed by a car dealer named Real Couetté. But Couetté and Thompson had a falling-out, and the two groups went their own ways.

And, for a few years, the Conservatives tried to operate with a non-Quebec leader (Robert Stanfield) and a Quebec lieutenant, but that never quite worked either.

There has been no political longevity in Canada since 1968 under a prime minister from the west or anywhere else — except Quebec. And there were enough tries: John Turner, Joe Clark, and Kim Campbell. From this perspective, it is safe to say that Preston Manning is prepared for whatever comes. Like his father, he takes the position that he does not need the job, but he is prepared to do it if God and the people want him to serve.

There are several possible scenarios: Reform could form the government, replace the Bloc as the official opposition, stay right where it is, or slide into the oblivion that prairie-based populist parties have entered in the past. What would have to change for any one of the scenarios to take place?

Forming the government: The Liberals would have to lose a lot of popularity, especially in Ontario. If that province's economy continues to improve and its voters figure that Mike Harris's kind of fiscal conservatism really works, they might say it is time to give Reform a try. Reform would have to retain or improve its present strength in the west, as well as pick up a lot of support in Ontario, to form the government.

Moving into official opposition: The Bloc would have to weaken, with the Liberals picking up strength in Quebec to compensate for some Reform gains in Ontario. The proponents of a strategic alliance between Reformers and Tories point out that it might best work in Ontario, with the Tories focusing on the urban areas and the Reform focusing on the hinterland.

Staying where it is or sliding back: Each situation could result from a Conservative resurgence. If voters in Ontario and Alberta decide that Jean Charest is more likely to give them Mike Harris- or Ralph Klein-type government in Ottawa, that resurgence could happen. But it is a long shot.

Like his father had, Preston Manning has some hidden strengths that come from his faith and the relationships that surround it. And if he and *Maclean's* are right, there are a lot of people in Canada who believe in the implications of Manning-style faith. That is why I was motivated to write *Like Father, Like Son.*

There is just one more possible scenario. Jean Charest is one generation removed from Preston Manning. Suppose he starts to gain ground in his home province, restoring some of the Tory strength of earlier years. Consider the possibilities if the Albertan and the Quebecker, sharing similar populist, fiscally responsible, compassionate, social conservative values, could build together. That is a long shot too, because Canada's track record says it can't be done. But the comments that Jean Charest made in the House of Commons, in tribute to Ernest Manning, hint at the possibility of something that would excite many voters. It would be reconciliation in action, and it could bring about the new Canada, the object of Preston Manning's political passion.

Works Consulted

Barr, John J. *The Dynasty: The Rise and Fall of Social Credit in Alberta*. Toronto: McClelland, 1974.

Bentall, Shirley. *From Buckboard to Brotherhood: The Baptist Churches in Calgary*. Calgary: Century Calgary, 1975.

Braid, Don, and Sydney Sharp. *Storming Babylon: Preston Manning and the Rise of the Reform Party*. Toronto: Key Porter, 1992.

Dobbin, Murray. *Preston Manning and the Reform Party*. Toronto: Lorimer, 1991.

Elliott, David R., and Iris Miller. *Bible Bill: A Biography of William Aberhart*. Edmonton: Reidmore, 1987.

Finkel, Alvin. *The Social Credit Phenomenon in Alberta*. Toronto: U of Toronto P, 1989.

Greenspon, Edward. *Double Vision: The Inside Story of the Liberals in Power*. Toronto: Doubleday, 1996.

Hansard Commons Debates, 21 Mar. 1996.

Harrison, Trevor. *Of Passionate Intensity: Right-Wing Populism and the Reform Party of Canada*. Toronto: U of Toronto P, 1995.

Hooke, A.J. *30 + 5: I Know, I Was There*. Edmonton: Self-published, 1971.

Irving, John A. *The Social Credit Movement in Alberta*. Toronto: U of Toronto P, 1959.

Mann, William E. *Sect, Cult and Church in Alberta*. Toronto: U of Toronto P, 1955.

Manning Consultants Ltd. "Proposal for the Creation of a Western-Based Political Party to Run Candidates in the 1988 Federal Election." Unpublished ts. Nov. 1986.

Manning, Ernest C. "The Concerns of Our Times." Tss. of 1984 eight-part sermon series from the *National Bible Hour*, as well as other tss. provided by Global Outreach Mission, St. Catharines, ON.

Manning, Preston. *The New Canada*. Toronto: Macmillan, 1992.

McPherson, C.B. *Democracy in Alberta: Social Credit and the Party System*. Toronto: U of Toronto P, 1970.

Official dedication of Global Outreach Mission's Ernest C. Manning Building, with Preston Manning as guest speaker. Videocassette. Edmonton: Kennedy Recordings, 1996.

The Reform Party. Videocassette [a two-part presentation on Vision TV, produced for the Evangelical Fellowship of Canada, with Preston Manning as guest]. Markham, ON: Winbourne Productions, 1991.

Thompson, Robert N. *House of Minorities*, Burlington, ON: Welch, 1990.

University of Alberta Archives. *E.C. Manning Fonds*, Accession No. 81–32.

Zeman, Jarold, ed. *Baptists in Canada: Search for Identity Amidst Diversity*. Burlington, ON: Welch, 1980.

imprimerie   gagné ltée